THE CARE AND FEEDING OF HEALTHY KIDS

Sara Sloan

 ACCENT BOOKS
Denver, CO 80215

ACCENT BOOKS

A division of Accent Publications, Inc.
12100 West Sixth Avenue
P.O. Box 15337
Denver, Colorado 80215

Library of Congress Catalog Card Number 85-071040

ISBN 0-89636-162-4

DEDICATED

In love and devotion
to my
mother and father
who gave me such
a
super beginning

ACKNOWLEDGMENTS

To my husband, Bill, for his love, encouragement and patience while this book was being written.

To all the teachers, moms and dads in my nutrition classes who taught me that kids are healthier and happier when nutrition comes naturally.

FOREWORD

Sara Sloan has captured all the evidence for why we should be feeding our children better. Good nutrition is a lifetime investment.

Pregnancy is like a launching pad for the rest of a child's life. Stress or inadequate nutrition during a pregnancy will deplete the mother and the baby of a number of key nutrients and can cause the baby to be born with allergies, irritability and generalized surliness. During those nine crucial months, a baby must receive good nutrition from the mother.

Continuing from infancy to feeding a school-aged child, Sara's expertise reaches its zenith. The evidence is in: Diet does affect the behavior and learning of children as well as adults. Sara's well-documented and easy-to-follow methods of eating give the reader everything needed to implement a program of healthful eating.

There are many other books which tell us to eat better foods, but THE CARE AND FEEDING OF HEALTHY KIDS makes the reader an instant expert with knowledgeable reasons for nutritious eating. Parents should buy this book and then march into the schools to get the principals and cooks to follow it!

Or, maybe someone should promote a federal department of *eating* and get Sara to be in charge. She knows what she is talking about. We can all benefit by listening and then doing something about it.

Lendon H. Smith, M.D.
Portland, Oregon

OTHER BOOKS BY THE AUTHOR

A Guide for Nutra Lunches and Natural Foods

From Classroom to Cafeteria

Yuk to Yum Snacks

Children Cook Naturally

The Brown Bag Cookbook

CONTENTS

Introduction

While teaching and feeding over 109 million school children in 31 years as director of school nutrition programs, I have had numerous opportunities for observing eating habits of children that range from finicky, picky, allergic and wacky to the healthy.

Mention the word *cholesterol* and most people think of the over 40 group. Yet autopsies in this country on young children who die from accidental causes show heart disease beginning at very early ages. There is growing evidence that the high fat diet of most Americans is related to the increase of certain forms of cancer and heart disease. Obesity affects one out of four school children due to the non-stop consumption of junk food. The time to attack these dreaded killers is before they start by using a program of parental prevention.

Hyperactivity, obesity, fatigue, allergies, tooth decay, anemia, chronic infections, as well as high levels of cholesterol in children are linked to the consumption of too many calories in saturated fat, sugar-rich, salty, and caffeine-laced foods. Yet seductive television advertising, fast food establishments with their kid-appealing tote boxes, peer pressure, vending machines—even the Easter bunny and Santa Claus—contribute to cravings for Marshmallow Fairies. When visions of sugarplums, shakes or fries are dancing in your head, apples and carrot sticks are less inviting.

Children come to school these days wearing house keys due to lifestyle changes in their homes. Many are responsible for preparing their own breakfast, after-school snack, and often their evening meal. Left on their own, most choose refined and sugary cereals, white bread and jelly, cookies, chocolate and soft drinks—all mood changing foods which cause undesirable behavior such as aggressiveness, hostility, restlessness, short attention span, excessive talking, poor writing, and a constant craving for sweets.

More and more scientific research is surging forth regarding the importance of nutrition to health, fitness and longevity. The payoff of a healthier life is priceless. But food education is not a "one time thing." It is a continuous teaching process—for better or for worse—by moms and dads, grandparents, teachers, big brothers, coaches, nurses, dentists—and even pediatricians. Everyone responsible for the nurturing of children should create happy learning experiences for them early—as someone has said, even before they leave the delivery table.

Few children can be trusted to make healthy food choices on their own and choose what's good for them. How can parents teach their children healthy eating habits that will last a lifetime? How can nutritionally-concerned parents make their influence felt with the teachers and cafeteria managers at their children's school?

The suggestions in this book come from personal experience as a mother, grandmother and teacher who has spent many hours in nutrition seminars with moms and dads. It is possible to wean kids from junk food painlessly, gradually, one step at a time—and with love.

Nutritional abuse of children is a subtle form of child abuse. All children deserve the priceless gift of health. Should we not try to give it to them?

Sara Sloan
Atlanta, Georgia

1
Eating for Health

Are you the steward of your family's health, Christian parent, that God has called you to be? As Christians our bodies are the temple of the Holy Spirit and He lives within us (I Corinthians 6:19,20). When we think of what God has done for us, it doesn't seem too much to ask that we glorify Him with every part of the bodies He has made. Everything we do must glorify God—even what we eat and drink (I Corinthians 10:31).

The health of American families is being sabotaged by the devitalized, fake, highly processed, chemical-laden foods passed off on them by some manufacturers. Children today come to school programmed to eat "burgers, fries and shakes." When some second-graders were asked recently to name the most nutritious foods, the answers were those of fast foods shown on television!

Although heart attacks usually don't occur until ages 40 to 60, research shows that the progressive build-up of plaque in arteries begins as early as age three. In elementary school, 4 percent of the children have elevated blood pressure; 25 to 30 percent have dangerously high cholesterol levels; 19 percent are overweight; 60 percent have at least one heart disease factor; and almost half have tried smoking.

The time to attack cardiovascular disease is before it starts. A healthy lifestyle and nourishing whole foods provided naturally by God can help everyone live an abundant, healthier life. Think of the magnificent array of colors, tastes, textures and smells of whole, fresh foods that have come from the hand of God. The Creator said to the first man Adam, *"I give you every seed-bearing plant on the face of the whole earth and every tree that has fruit with seed in it. They will be yours for food"* (Genesis 1:29, NIV). God's original plan for eating is still the best plan for us today.

The old cliche is even more true in these days—you are what you eat. The foods on our plates can determine how long and how well we will live. Food choices directly affect body growth, development and energy levels to think, play, work and feel. Healthy foods are not necessarily bland or boring. Eating healthfully doesn't mean giving up every favorite food. But kids can discover that they can live quite happily even without Kool-Aid.

With one-parent households on the increase and more than 60 percent of American moms in the labor force, one of the most frequently asked questions is, "How do I provide my family with tasty, nutritious, low-cost meals?"

The best answer is to get kids hooked on healthy food by putting into effect in your home a "Parental Prevention Program" that suits your situation and involves everyone in the family. Food education that helps to nourish the physical, mental and spiritual needs of a child creates healthy attitudes that last a lifetime. How?

First, *parents must set a healthy example.* One cannot talk with a forked tongue when trying to influence others to kick sugar, fat, salt and caffeine. When parents choose nutritious foods themselves, it becomes easier to make believers out of the kids. The prime time when kids imitate their parents and peers is between the ages of two and six. If kids see Mom and Dad grab a handful of cookies every pass through the kitchen, munch on potato chips while watching television, or have ice cream for dessert every evening, so will the kids. When parents use the car to visit a friend one block away, children learn early that feet weren't made for walking. When Dad's main interest in sports is watching it on TV, kids become armchair athletes and their most strenuous exercise is reaching for pretzels. Body language is a powerful teacher.

Too many moms and dads begin the day with sweet rolls, doughnuts and coffee for breakfast, or even skip breakfast altogether. Then they present a fatigued, poorly nourished body for God to use in whatever job He has set before them. Part of our stewardship as Christians is to be physically fit, sparkling with energy and ready for God's call. This dimension is often neglected by many Christians.

What kind of food messages do you send to your family? What do they see when they open the refrigerator? Children will imitate the undesirable as well as the good. When Dad reaches for the salt shaker, he teaches his children to do the same. Dad cannot munch on fast food burgers or fatty fries without providing the same option to the kids. Many times parents justify their own sweet tooth by blaming the children for supermarket baskets loaded with ice cream, cookies and cakes. But if parents enjoy a variety of interesting, nourishing foods every day, so will the children.

The second step is to *get acquainted with the fundamental nutrients essential for optimal health.* There is no magic pill or superfood that contains all of your body's necessary nutrients. Healthful living requires a knowledgeable combination of foods to provide the needed nutrients. Each nutrient has a vital function to perform and each is related. Nutrients work together in your body just as a symphony orchestra does. Each piece is dependent upon the other to provide body cells with balanced nourishment. When even one nutrient is missing, body processes are impaired and we do not function at our best.

When planning meals and snacks for your family, learn how to do a balancing act with proteins, carbohydrates, fats, and the protective foods.

PROTEINS—The Body's Building Blocks

Protein is an essential nutrient present in every cell of the body. Protein's major function is to build, repair, regulate and renew the heart, brain, internal organs, blood, eyes, muscles, skin, hair and nails. Protein is also involved in the formation of many essential body chemicals, enzymes and hormones. Protein is needed not only for initial growth, but also to help form new tissues and repair worn-out ones.

If you are showing signs of sagging facial muscles, crepey eyelids, flabby arms or dull-looking hair, maybe you need to do a protein check. When combined with vitamin C, protein forms collagen which is essential for keeping skin tissues and muscles firm.

Protein is composed of amino acids. Scientists tell us there are basically 22 amino acids. Nine are called essential amino acids, since the body cannot make them and they must be provided daily from the food we eat. These nine amino acids are essential for growth and maintenance. The other amino acids can be manufactured by the body.

The nine essential amino acids are: phenylalanine, tryptophan, methionine, histidine, valine, leucine, isoleucine, threonine and lysine. These are called complete proteins and are of animal origin. Incomplete proteins are found in vegetables and plant products, which, when skillfully combined to complement each other, furnish complete amino acid balance.

ANIMAL PROTEIN

Included in this category are meats, poultry, fish, cheese, eggs and dairy products. Recommended are fish, chicken or turkey (minus the skin which contains most of the fat); lean beef (occasionally) with the fat removed; low-fat skim milk, cheeses and other dairy products. Low-fat products, however, are not recommended for children under two years of age. They may be substituted after age two. Eggs are also a valuable source of protein. The whites contain 98 percent protein with no fat or cholesterol. The fat in any egg recipe can be cut by using one whole egg and two egg whites. Also, turkey minus the skin (and fat) has 46 percent protein compared to chicken with 41 percent.

Darker turkey meat contains more fat than the white meat.

Several kinds of fish contain less than 5 percent fat. These include bass, haddock, rockfish, shrimp, cod, halibut, salmon, swordfish, flounder, red snapper, scallops, trout, and tuna. (Tuna in oil has 34 percent protein and 64 percent fat. Drain off all the oil and the protein jumps to 58 percent. If you buy tuna in oil, rinse it lightly in cold water to remove the oil. But tuna packed in water is a better nutrition buy.)

Liver should be included as an important source of protein. It is one of those superfoods that contains a broad spectrum of essential nutrients. Others are whole grains, dark green or deep yellow vegetables or fruits, and dry beans. One major hotel restaurant in Atlanta serves liver on their gourmet buffet so tastefully prepared that only liver-lovers "know for sure."

Liver is an organ meat and thus is not advisable for those on a low-cholesterol diet, but otherwise the smorgasbord of nutrients in liver include:

LIVER'S NUTRIENTS	AMOUNTS (in a 4 oz. serving of cooked beef liver)
Calories	229
Protein	26.4 grams
Fat	10.6 grams
Cholesterol	372 milligrams
Sodium	184 milligrams
Vitamin A	53,500 I.U. (hamburger contains 0)
Vitamin B_1 (thiamin)	.26 milligrams (hamburger contains .08)

Vitamin B$_2$ (riboflavin)	4.19 milligrams (hamburger contains 1.19)
Vitamin B$_{12}$	35 milligrams (hamburger contains 2)
Niacin	16.5 milligrams
Calcium	11 milligrams
Vitamin C	27 milligrams
Iron	8.8 milligrams
Phosphorous	476 milligrams
Potassium	380 milligrams

(From *Handbook of The Nutritional Content of Foods*, United States Department of Agriculture.)

VEGETABLE PROTEIN

Included in this category are seeds, nuts, whole grains, legumes, pastas, dried peas and beans. (Legumes include soybeans, peanuts, black-eyed peas, kidney beans, chickpeas, navy peas, and lima beans.) By combining certain incomplete proteins in such forms as pizza on whole wheat crust, brown rice and beans, or peanut butter on whole grain bread, you can form a complete protein. Combine brown rice with wheat, dry beans or peas; or legumes with corn, wheat, barley, oats, millet or seeds.

Vegetable proteins are a nutritious bargain—less expensive, low in fat with no cholesterol, and contain valuable fiber as well as the complex carbohydrates. At least two nights a week stretch your food dollars by using heart-saving extenders such as vegetables, brown rice, pasta, eggs or tofu. Tofu, which is soybean cheese, has been used in Oriental cooking for thousands of years, and with a little experimentation, it becomes a healthy alternative to meat. Tofu is inexpensive, contains no cholesterol, is low in calories (80 calories in four ounces), and weighs in at about nine grams of protein in a two-inch square.

How much protein is needed? Americans in general consume too much protein and waste their food budget by eating more than is needed by the body. Excess protein is converted into urea which is excreted by the kidneys. This is not only wasteful and stressful to the kidneys, but it is also fattening and could present a health hazard.

Ideally, your daily meal plan should be divided into 15 to 20 percent protein, 55 to 70 percent complex carbohydrates, and 20 to 25 percent fat (20 percent fat is preferable).

In general, infants need three times the amount of protein, pound for pound, as adults with the need being the greatest during the first six months of life. Protein requirements decline as one gets older, but quality protein is needed by those past 50.

The Food and Nutrition Board of the National Academy of Sciences recommends the following daily allowances of protein:

	Age	Protein (grams per pound)
Children	1-3	0.81
	4-6	0.68
	7-10	0.55
	11-14	0.45
	15-18	0.39
Adults	19 and over	0.36
	Pregnant	0.62
	Nursing	0.53

For example: to determine the needs...
    For a 5 year old who weighs 50 pounds:
       $0.68 \times 50 = 34$ grams
    For a 12 year old who weighs 110 pounds:
       $0.45 \times 110 = 49.5$ grams
    For a pregnant woman who weighs 125 pounds:
       $0.62 \times 125 = 77.5$ grams

CARBOHYDRATES—The Fuelish Choice

It is no longer out of style to be unrefined. In fact, going "with the grains" is no longer just "for the birds." Carbohydrates are the body's major source of energy. They are especially important because once digested, some produce glucose which is an essential food for the brain.

Carbohydrates are not fattening since, ounce for ounce, they have the same calories as protein—four calories per gram. Complex carbohydrates can actually help you lose weight since they are a rich source of nutrients for appetite satiation and chewiness. For example, fruits are packed with vitamins, minerals, fiber and valuable carbohydrates while at the same time satisfying a craving for sweets.

All carbohydrates are not created equal, though. Some have many of the beneficial nutrients refined out of them by food manufacturers, leaving behind fake foods and empty calories. When whole wheat flour is processed to white flour, at least 80 percent of the fiber is lost as well as other valuable nutrients. As a general rule, remember that the less refining of the grains, the better for health. To get the most nutrients for your money, purchase whole grain breads from stone-ground flour. The next best choice would be 100 percent whole grain bread. But be sure to read labels for ingredients. Some dark breads are actually colored with caramel.

SIMPLE AND COMPLEX CARBOHYDRATES

What are the different carbohydrates? The *simple* carbohydrates are the sugars which can be broken down into glucose quickly. Starches are called *complex* carbohydrates and break down into glucose more slowly. These provide sustained energy over a longer period of time.

NATURAL AND PROCESSED CARBOHYDRATES

Natural carbohydrates, both simple and complex, are found in whole foods such as fruits, vegetables, nuts, seeds or whole grains as close to the way they come from the earth as possible. All of these contain fiber mingled with other nutrients. This is the tough "overcoat" found on the outside of grains, seeds, in vegetables, skins of potatoes, pears and apples, the outside dark green of lettuce (which is usually discarded), celery and nuts.

Processed or refined carbohydrates (i.e. man-made) are relatively low in nutrients compared to the large amount of calories they contain. Some of these are jelly, cakes, cookies, pies, bakery goods, crackers, soft drinks, convenience foods or artificial foods.

Processed foods contain little or no fiber. They are absorbed into the blood stream quickly and temporarily flood the body with more fuel than is needed. This causes the pancreas to produce more and more insulin to remove the excess sugar. The insulin's overreaction drives the blood sugar level down which results in low blood sugar and a vicious cycle is established.

Too much refined sugar contributes to obesity, tooth decay, diabetes and even heart disease. It depletes the body's store of vitamin B and is addictive. Even those who "don't eat sweets" cannot avoid it because it is hidden in processed foods. Dextrose, another word for sugar, is even in table salt so that it will pour easily.

In nature, sugar always occurs with protective fiber, vitamins and minerals. Looking at a banana day after day may not be very exciting unless you learn to see it as a potential weapon against heart attack, anemia or cancer. That apple a day may not keep the tumor away, but studies show that your odds for preventing certain diseases are much better by eating fruit.

The National Academy of Sciences' Committee on Diet, Nutrition and Cancer, the American Diabetes Association and the American Heart Association all endorse eating fruit not only to replace refined, fatty desserts but for the protective dietary fibers, particularly pectin, supplied in fruit. Pectin dramatically lowers blood cholesterol, increases bulk in the stomach which helps to prevent overeating, and the broomlike fibers ease digestion and elimination. Sugars in fruit are digested more slowly and do not cause the yo-yo effect of white sugar on the body's metabolism. Some carbonated sodas contain as much as 38 grams of sugar. To obtain this amount from food one would have to eat: 4 apples, 4 pears and a 7-ounce banana.

RECOMMENDED WHOLE FOOD CARBOHYDRATES

Breads and Cereals

Bread has been the staff of life for thousands of years. The Bible records instructions for the children of Israel as to the kinds of bread they were to eat: *"Take thou also unto thee wheat, and barley, and beans, and lentiles, and millet, and fitches [herbs], and put them in one vessel, and make thee bread thereof..."* (Ezekiel 4:9).

That advice is still valid today. A healthy diet should include whole grain breads, cereals, rolls, tortillas, noodles, pasta (whole wheat pasta or "green" pasta is more nutritious than plain pasta), brown rice, pancakes, oats, millet, barley, bulgur or buckwheat.

Dr. James Anderson, an endocrinologist at the University of Kentucky, recommends eating 1½ ounces of oat bran daily or enough for ½ cup of cereal or two oat bran muffins. Hot cereal made from oatmeal or oat bran reduces fats and cholesterol more effectively than any other grain because whole oats such as steel cut oats or rolled oats soak up fatty proteins in the intestines and carry them out of the body.

Genesis 25:30-34 tells us that Esau sold his birthright to Jacob for a "pottage of lentiles" (a pod-like leguminous plant). Nutritionally it wasn't a bad deal. Lentils contain no fat while providing more protein and more vitamins A, C and B than sirloin steak. They also contain calcium, phosphorous, and iron.

Potatoes

These healthy meals-in-a-peel are filling and a great fast food substitute. Baked potatoes make a super one-dish food loaded with protein, iron, B vitamins, phosphorous, vitamin C, magnesium, copper, iodine and folacin. A plain, medium-sized potato has only 90 to 110 calories and can be served with a variety of toppings for a perfect meal.

MENU IDEAS

For hot toppers: Try steamed broccoli and low-fat cheese, ham, poached eggs, Swiss cheese, chili with beans, chopped spinach, Cheddar cheese, diced eggs, sauteed mushrooms, or mixed vegetables and sesame seeds.

For cold toppers: Use mushrooms, artichoke hearts, Parmesan cheese, avocado wedges, tomato cubes, onion, plain yogurt, taco sauce, tuna salad, tomato and steamed green beans, diced tomato with grated mozzarella cheese and jalapeno peppers, chopped cucumbers with yogurt and dill, or low-fat cottage cheese and fresh chives.

Remember to scrub rather than peel your potatoes since many nutrients are in the potato skin or just under the skin.

Sweet potatoes are not related to the white potato but are an excellent nutrition bargain. They are high in vitamins A and C, and low in calories.

Beans, Beans, Beans

Dried beans of every origin are a double duty food because they are both a vegetable and a meat substitute due to their high protein content. All beans are created equal, calorically speaking (about 95 calories per ounce, dried), and have about the same protein content (6 grams per ounce). Beans have no fat and are high in fiber. You will save cash and calories when beans are on the menu.

Yellow Corn

This vegetable is a superstar as a source of energy, vitamin A and vitamin C. Popcorn, a relative of yellow corn, was first introduced by the Pilgrims who served it at their Thanksgiving meal. Popcorn addicts enjoy this nutritious snack which is low in calories (depending on what you put on it) and yet high in fiber. Pop your popcorn in a hot-air popper and enjoy even more calorie savings.

1 cup hot-air popped popcorn = 50 calories
1 cup popcorn with oil and salt = 81 calories

Next time you want to snack, remember that two quarts of popcorn have fewer calories than 25 potato chips.

Fruits and Vegetables

Both fruits and vegetables should be eaten fresh and whole whenever possible. The closer fruits and vegetables are to their natural state, the higher their vitamin and mineral content. Maximum nutritional mileage is gained when fruits and vegetables are eaten raw or lightly steamed because valuable vitamins and minerals—elusive potassium in particular—are destroyed in boilng. If you do boil your vegetables, always save the liquid for soups.

Statistics show that one out of every three Americans will develop cancer at some time. The National Cancer Institute says that diet may be responsible for 60 percent of all cancers among women and 40 percent among men. Many prestigious scientific journals are saying the same thing regarding the role of food in relationship to developing cancer. Eating certain foods every day and avoiding others may help you change those statistics and pay off in healthier lives for you and your family.

FATS

Fat produces a concentrated form of energy, provides essential fatty acids, cushions our vital organs, and is a carrier of the fat soluble vitamins A, D, E and K. Fat is high in calories, yielding 9 calories per gram. (Protein and carbohydrates yield 4 calories per gram.)

Surprisingly, only one tablespoon of fat is needed per person per day. Unfortunately, most adults consume eight to ten tablespoons of fat a day. Much fat is hidden in processed and refined foods. Reducing fat intake is one of the most important steps in eating for better health.

SATURATED FATS

Saturated fats come from animal origins such as meats, milk, butter and cheese and are usually solid at room temperature. But coconut and palm oil from vegetable sources also contain high amounts of saturated fats. These oils should be avoided. All saturated fats should be strictly limited.

HYDROGENATED FATS

These are 20th century fats that have become saturated through hydrogenation (the addition of hydrogen to an unsaturated organic compound). You will find hydrogenated fats in the vegetable shortenings, lard and hard margarines usually used to make commercial snack foods. It is also found in commercial salad dressings, breads, cakes, pies, cookies and processed convenience foods. Avoid all partially or fully hydrogenated oils, fats or products containing them. The hydrogen prevents the body from absorbing the fat soluble vitamins.

UNSATURATED FATS

Unsaturated fats are usually liquid at room temperature and are found in vegetable and seed oils as well as most nuts. Linseed oil tops the health list along with safflower, corn, sesame, wheat germ, soy, sunflower, and almond.

Unsaturated oils such as safflower and corn are used in making soft margarines. These are recommended because they have little or no cholesterol. (Cholesterol is a fat substance in our blood, and our bodies cannot function normally without it; but, when the amount gets too high, the cholesterol may deposit as fatty plaque on the walls of our arteries and lead to the disease atherosclerosis, hardening of the arteries.) We are often warned to avoid saturated fats as much as possible because these tend to increase cholesterol in the blood. It is best to major on unsaturated fats or foods known to be low in cholesterol.

According to Dr. William Castelli, director of the world-renowned Framingham Heart Study in Framingham, Massachusetts, it is easy to tell which brands of margarines have little or no cholesterol. Just look at the label of ingredients. If the first word is "liquid," it's good;

if the first word is "partly," it's not good. If the first word is "water," then it's a low fat margarine and is excellent.

Fish has long been called a brain food but now is touted as "heart food" also. It is low in cholesterol, fat and calories but high in healthy fish oils. The fish oils we should be eating and feeding to our children include those from salmon, mackerel, cod, mullet, Norwegian or Maine canned sardines, rockfish, sea trout, perch, red snapper, halibut and swordfish. White meat albacore tuna fish packed in oil or water is of medium fatty acid content. Other kinds of canned tuna have these valuable fatty acids removed in processing.

Fish oils are extremely rich in unsaturated fats and are found in high levels in cold-water fish. Researchers are finding that fish oils:

● Help lower cholesterol, blood fats and triglyceride levels.

● Help prevent blood clots.

● May retard the slow buildup of artery clogging fats.

● May help relieve some skin problems such as eczema and psoriasis.

● May help combat inflammatory conditions such as arthritis.

● May aid brain development.

Adapted from *Fish for the Heart* by Tom Hager, *American Health*, April 1985.

PROTECTIVE FOODS

Some of the following protective foods, rich in vitamin A, vitamin C, selenium, fiber and water should be a part of the diet each day:

VITAMINS A AND C

The vital nutrient found abundantly in deep yellow, orange and dark green fruits and vegetables is a substance called beta-carotene. As the body needs it, it converts this compound to vitamin A which bolsters the body's defense against germs. Beta-carotene rich foods include acorn squash, apricots, broccoli, butternut squash, cantaloupe, carrots, collard greens, hubbard squash, kale, peaches, prunes, pumpkin, spinach (cooked), sweet potatoes, tomatoes, and zucchini.

Vitamin C sources include all citrus fruits, as well as broccoli, brussels sprouts, cabbage, cauliflower, dark leafy vegetables, melons, sweet red peppers, and tomatoes.

The beta-carotene foods provide vim, vigor and vitamins A and C, but with them be sure to include each day one or more of the detoxifying cruciferous vegetables from the cabbage or mustard family. These include cabbage, brussels sprouts, swiss chard, cauliflower, and mustard. These valuable vegetables increase the body's production of cancer-inhibiting enzymes.

Actually, the latest weapon in the war on cancer may be in the vegetable bins of most American refrigerators. Substances called dithiolthiones, composed of sulphur and carbon, exist in large quantities in cabbage family vegetables—the cruciferous vegetables. These substances not only work as anti-cancer compounds but may also protect against radiation from X rays, video games, television and radiation treatments. Crisp shredded cabbage added to all green salads or sandwiches makes a potent health preservative.

SELENIUM

Selenium is a mineral deserving attention also as a protective nutrient. It contains anti-cancer characteristics and only a minute trace is needed to get the job done, so include fish, seafood, liver, brewer's yeast, bran, wheat germ, whole grains, and a variety of vegetables in your diet to be sure that trace is available to your body.

FIBER

For years the forgotten nutrient, fiber is now reported by many scientists as valuable in reducing the incidence of obesity, heart disease, diabetes, colon cancer, diverticulosis, constipation, hemorrhoids, hiatus hernia and varicose veins. It should be featured as one of the protective foods. Dr. Denis Burkitt, a member of the British Medical Research Council and co-discoverer of the importance of fiber in the diet, states that the amount of fiber listed on the back of that box of breakfast cereal or loaf of bread is misleading.

Processed or man-made foods do not contain much fiber. Whole meal flour, for instance, contains all of the ground grain including bran, wheat germ and endosperm, while processed flour retains only the endosperm, losing bran and wheat germ.

Rural Africans—healthy, non-obese, and virtually free of colon cancer, coronary heart disease and diabetes—consume 25 grams of fiber in cereal, 6 grams in potatoes and legumes, and 5.3 grams in fruits and vegetables. Americans take in only about 6.4 grams of fiber—0.5 grams of cereals, 0.9 grams of potatoes and legumes, and 5.0 grams in fruits and vegetables.

There are several ways fiber can be added to a family's meals.

1. Include daily: 1 cup of whole grain cereal, brown rice or the equivalent; 2 slices of whole grain bread (wheat oats, rye, barley, corn), and 3 to 5 servings of fruits and vegetables (as many raw as possible).

2. Add wheat germ, bran or oatmeal to sauces, baked goods, meatloaf, spaghetti sauce or soups. (Be sure to start out gradually when adding miller's bran to your eating plan. Don't overload all at once. Start with 1 or 2 teaspoons and increase to 2 tablespoons a day.)

3. Substitute toasted oats, grapenut flakes, raisins, figs, dates or prunes in recipes calling for chocolate chips.

4. Nibble on whole grain cereals, wheat, rye or bran crackers.

5. Top salads with a sprinkling of nuts, seeds, spoon-size shredded wheat or cooked dried beans.

6. For a fast fiber booster, mix unprocessed bran, oats, or wheat bran flakes to pancake mix, bread crumbs, ground beef, and all bread toppings for baked desserts.

Be sure to include plenty of liquids when increasing fiber in your diet.

WATER

Drink a reasonable amount of liquid every day—no less than 5 or 6 glasses unless strenuously exercising or working, and then drink more. But drink the "real thing," rather than sugary drinks. They make you thirstier by dehydrating the body during digestion.

Water, according to the American College of Sports Medicine, is the best thirst quencher before, during and after strenuous exercise. One should drink two cups of liquid for every pound of body weight lost in perspiration.

What kind of water should you drink? Depending on the quality of the water where you live, you may need to invest in a special filter for the tap or look for other sources, such as:

Spring water. Once you taste the fresh mineral water from an underground mountain spring, it may be impossible to settle for tap water again. If you do not own a mountain, bottled spring or mineral water, complete with a stand and dispenser, can be delivered to your home from a water supplier.

Distilled water. Distilled water loses its natural mineral content in the distilling process. Some physicians, however, recommend distilled water for salt-free or low-salt diets. When using distilled water, minerals should be monitored carefully.

Sparkling water. This can be naturally or artificially carbonated. Natural carbonation occurs when water flows through limestone or other carbonate rocks. Artificial carbonation occurs by adding carbon dioxide to water. Keep sparkling water tightly capped or the "fizzle" disappears.

Summertime for kids usually means endless thirst with the accompanying parental problem of what to serve for thirst-quenchers that are nutritious, good tasting, easily prepared and inexpensive. Drinking for health means more than diet sodas or caffeine-charged colas or even iced tea. Refresh your children and adults with water. It is inexpensive and easily available. You may want to keep a kid-sized container in the refrigerator with a special cup for each youngster.

Eating water is also a good idea. Give kids fresh high-water content foods like cantaloupe, cucumbers, watermelons, tomatoes, lettuce, and zucchini to supplement fluids. Green grapes, melon cubes or strawberries can be threaded on a wooden skewer as a treat. Nuggets of fresh fruit frozen in ice cubes add a touch of summer to any drink. Slices of peaches, melon or strawberry cubes dropped into a tall glass of spring or mineral water liven up any hot, sluggish afternoon.

The following list can be used as a guide in selecting protective foods for your family's meals.

PROTECTIVE FOODS

FOOD	PORTION	VITAMIN A Int'l Units	VITAMIN C (milligrams)
Beef liver	3 oz.	45,390	23
Beet greens	1 cup	7,400	22
Broccoli (fresh)	1 stalk	4,500	162
Broccoli (frozen)	1 stalk	570	22
Cantaloupe	½ melon	9,240	90
Carrots, raw	1 medium	7,930	6
Carrots, cooked	1 cup	16,280	9
Cabbage, Chinese (cooked/drained)	1 cup	5,270	26
Collard greens (cooked/drained from raw)	1 cup	14,820	144
Collard greens (frozen/chopped)	1 cup	11,560	56
Dandelion greens (cooked/drained)	1 cup	12,290	19
Endive, curly (includes escarole)	1 cup	1,650	5
Kale (cooked/drained from raw)	1 cup	9,130	130

Kale (frozen/leaf)	1 cup	10,660	49
Oranges	1 medium	260	66
Orange juice	1 cup	540	120
Oysters	13 to 19	740	0
Pumpkin, canned	1 cup	15,680	12
Spinach (raw/chopped)	1 cup	4,460	28
Spinach (cooked/ drained from raw)	1 cup	14,580	50
Spinach (frozen/chopped)	1 cup	16,200	39
Squash, winter (all varieties)	1 cup	8,610	27
Sweet potatoes (baked in skin)	1 medium	9,230	25
(boiled in skin)	1 medium	11,940	26
Sweet potatoes, canned	1 medium	19,890	36
Tomatoes, fresh	1 medium	1,110	28
Tomatoes, canned	1 cup	2,170	41
Turnip greens (cooked/ drained from raw)	1 cup	8,270	68
Turnip greens (frozen/chopped)	1 cup	11,390	31

Table from United States Department of Agriculture, Home and Garden Bulletin No. 72, Superintendent of Documents, U.S. Government Printing Office, Washington, D.C. 20402, Revised April, 1981.

FOODS TO AVOID

Having looked closely at healthy foods, it's also important to be aware of foods to avoid. These include fats, too much protein, alcoholic beverages, mold on food, and cured or smoked meats. These meats contain the nutritionally dangerous nitrosamines and polycyclic aromatic hydrocarbons. Most importantly, limit—or eliminate—sugar. No doubt about it, sugar is our "good time" food. From birthday cakes to breaks with doughnuts, our associations with sugar are warm and loving. Desserts, however, probably cause more ill health than any other part of the American diet due to the high amount of refined sugar combined with high, saturated fat. And children love sweets. Eating desserts for health means serving sweetened desserts only occasionally, not on a regular basis. When there are no sweets in the house, kids will go for fruit. But fruit cannot compete against canned choco-pudding, candy sticks or cookies.

2
Busy Moms
and Healthy Meals

Any working mom knows that it's not just the cooking that's a chore. The menu planning, preparation, marketing, serving and the cleanup also take time. Even if mom can't come up with the answer to "What's for dinner?" she must come up with dinner. Preparing nutritious meals quickly and easily becomes easier when you follow the Boy Scouts' code—be prepared and organized.

But moms need to be aware of their own health patterns. How do you cope with your busy lifestyle? Take a quick inventory. Can't get going without your morning coffee? Do you need cola pickups throughout the day? Are you too busy to eat a real breakfast? Here are some facts to think about.

AVOID PERSONAL PITFALLS

Caffeine—a stimulant and diuretic—found in coffee, tea, and cola—has been called America's number 1 drug. Caffeine acts as a stimulant on the central nervous system and may be a contributor to all kinds of health problems including heart disease, cancer, fibrocystic breast disease, ulcers, and birth defects. Heavy consumption of coffee reduces the body's vitamin B_1 level (the nerve vitamin) by as much as 50 percent; for tea it increases to a possible 60 percent depletion. One can of cola in a young child is as potent as four cups of coffee in an adult.

Caffeine occurs in more than 60 species of plants. Primary examples are coffee beans, cola nuts, cocoa beans and tea leaves. Coffee is the nation's greatest source of caffeine, with soft drinks ranked in the number 2 spot, followed by tea and chocolate.

Caffeine Levels in Common Beverages

	Milligrams of Caffeine
COFFEE (5 ounces)	
Drip	146
Percolator	100
Instant	60
Decaffeinated	2
TEA (5 ounces)	
Black Tea brewed 5 minutes	50
Black Tea brewed 3 minutes	35
Black Tea brewed 1 minute	25
Green Tea	30
Instant Tea	30
CHOCOLATE	
Cocoa (6 ounces)	10
Hershey's Instant Chocolate (per tablespoon)	10
Carnation Instant Cocoa (per envelope)	13

Soda pop is undermining the health of millions due to major ingredients such as sugar, sodium, caffeine, phosphoric acids or phosphates, tannins, stannous chloride (for clarity in soft drinks), colorings, saccharin, sorbitol or aspartame for sweetening, citric acid, sodium benzoate, sulfur diozides or sulfites, propyl gallate, and EDTA (a preservative to extend the shelf life—ethylenediamine tetraacetic acid).

Soft drinks have displaced milk and fruit juice at an increasingly alarming rate. Between 1962 and 1983 the U.S. consumption of soft drinks increased from 32.6 percent to 55.1.

Now, diet soft drinks are rapidly replacing the regular sodas. Most diet drinks contain only one or two calories in a six ounce glass and some are sugar, sodium and caffeine free. But does that make them healthy?

Diet drinks contain carbonated water with added caramel color, phosphoric acid (which destroys tooth enamel, demineralizes calcium in bones and depletes zinc), sodium, saccharin or aspartame, citric acid and other chemical preservatives.

According to Dr. Neil Solomon of Johns Hopkins University School of Medicine there are two chemicals in diet sodas that can undo a diet—fluoride and chlorine. In excess, either one can replace the iodine in the thyroid gland. This results in a sluggish feeling and causes fewer calories to be burned.

Coffee, tea, colas and chocolate contain Xanthine stimulants which are powerful drugs. Caffeine provides a quick and temporary lift then drops you flat while ...

- increasing your heart rate.
- increasing your blood pressure.
- stressing your adrenal glands and causing them to release too much adrenalin.

- contributes to sleepiness, mood changes and anxiety.
- acts as a strong diuretic.

"Caffeine-aholics" have different individual levels of tolerance for the drug. Too many caffeine drinks have been linked to high cholesterol levels, fibrocystic disease and birth defects. One cup of coffee a day contains 125 milligrams of caffeine. Two hundred milligrams is considered a pharmacologically active dose, an amount which equals two cups of coffee or four cans of soft drinks. This level of caffeine intake can increase the risk of heart disease or hypertension in cases of obesity or iodine deficiency.

The amount of caffeine in tea, coffee, colas and chocolate depends upon the kind of bean used and the method of processing and preparing the product. The following chart lists the amount of caffeine in soft drinks and chocolate products.

Caffeine Levels in Soft Drinks

	Milligrams per 12 ounce can
Sugar-free Mr. Pibb	60
Mountain Dew	54
Mello Yello	52
Tab	46
Coca-Cola	45
Diet Coca-Cola	46
Shasta Cherry Cola	44
Shasta Diet Cola	44
SunKist Orange	40
Mr. Pibb	40
Dr. Pepper	40
Pepsi-Cola	38

Diet Pepsi	36
Pepsi Light	36
RC Cola	36
Diet Rite	36
Fresca	0
Fanta Drinks	0
Teem	0
Diet 7-Up	0
7-Up	0
RC 100	0
Canada Dry Ginger Ale	0
Orange Crush	0
Hires Root Beer	0

If you are considering taking the no-caffeine plunge, do it slowly. Gradual weaning will cause less pain. Try a mixture of regular and decaffeinated coffee or tea but choose a premium decaffeinated one. Bad coffee substitutes will send you right back to the old grind. Water-processed brands will give a fresher taste and fewer chemicals than chemically processed ones. They generally cost more so you use less.

When you get a craving for a warm drink try hot cider, flavored bouillon, Pero, Postum, herbed teas or Roastaroma (a blend of roasted barley, crystal malt, roasted carob, allspice and star anise). Hot molasses combined with ginger makes a healthy brew. *(Combine 2 tablespoons blackstrap molasses—a good source of B vitamins—with one-half teaspoon ginger. Slowly add 1½ cups of warm water. Boil for 1 minute.)*

The best thirst quencher, though, still contains no calories, caffeine or sugar. Water is more quickly absorbed into your system than juices or other drinks that contain sugar, glucose, sodium or potassium. And, water provides your body with valuable benefits essential to good health.

Stop and think before you drink. For instance: One cup of Gatorade contains 20 milligrams of potassium. One cup of orange juice contains 500 milligrams of potassium. On a hot day during two hours of gardening, bicycling or jogging, you may lose from 320 to 800 milligrams of potassium.

Commercially prepared drinks should be diluted with water to lower the concentrations of sugar being absorbed into the body—particularly during strenuous exercise when you perspire a lot.

STOKE UP FOR THE DAY

Breakfast is golden,
Lunch is silver
Dinner is lead.

Whoever put that jingle together knew that breakfast is the most important meal of the day. Research has shown that energy levels remain higher and mental productivity is greater when breakfast is eaten. Children cannot perform well at school or concentrate in class when there is no fuel in the tank. (Neither can teachers, moms or dads.)

Without a good breakfast, too many kids stop at the nearest store and load up on soft drinks, potato chips or candy bars on their way to school. Several years ago, in a survey of the breakfast habits of fourth graders, some admitted to taking just a vitamin tablet. Too many households operate on the eat-on-the-run plan or no plan at all for the morning nutrition stop.

Many think that breakfast can be skipped when counting calories, but this plan usually backfires when mid-morning hunger pangs strike. This frequently results in a quick raid on the nearest vending machine which is not usually filled with low-calorie munchies.

Breakfast has to have top priority for "get up and go" families. Breakfast doesn't have to be boring. Opening a box of cereal and pouring on milk is not etched in granite. Plan ahead for power-packed foods that include a good source of protein, whole grain breads or cereals, fruit and vegetables. Yes, veggies are "in" as breakfast food. Why not surprise the family with a steaming cup of vegetable soup or a mug of beans, prepared ahead and reheated for breakfast?

Serve Yourself Breakfast Bars are also immensely popular with most families (or schools). Breakfast bars can feature fresh fruit, whole grain muffins, yogurt and cheese.

Or try an Oatmeal Buffet. This features a steaming pot of oatmeal surrounded by crocks of healthy toppings such as seasonal fresh fruit, dried fruit, unsweetened granola, chopped nuts, coconut slivers, sesame and sunflower seeds, and yogurt.

Too many pre-packaged, pre-sweetened cereals are simply breakfast candies in disguise. Don't purchase cereals with sugar or fruit added. Read labels to avoid sugar, sodium and fat content. Add your own raisins to cereals—they are easier to chew.

Whether breakfast is carried, packed, or consumed while drying your hair, kick off with these starters:

Millet Cakes	Muffin Pizzas
Blender Smoothies	Fresh Fruit Kabobs
Rice Cakes	Tofu French Toast
Quiche Wedges	Breakfast Burgers
Rice Pudding	Nut-Milk Muesli
Tortilla Cheese Melt	Batter-up Waffles,

Mushroom Omelet
Peanut Butter Muffins
Mexican Salsa with Eggs
Apple-Bran Muffins
Breakfast Sundaes (layer
  sunflower or sesame
  seeds, fresh apples,
  bananas, nuts, oats,
  wheat germ and dates,
  top with yogurt)
Breakfast Sandwiches

Pancakes or Griddle
Cakes (can be frozen
ahead)
Croissants or Crepes
Sprouted Wheat or Rye
Berries
Sunburst Banana Granola
(sunflower and pumpkin
seeds, raisins, skim milk
powder, almonds, dates
and sesame seeds)

PREPARE FOR ACTION

Every mom who finds herself juggling car pools, Little League practice, late nights at the office, or any of the many hectic pressures of family life knows the answer to continued sanity is in being organized. The secret, of course, is in planning ahead. Some of the following planned strategies offer you imaginative options.

Plan Weekly Menus
Planning meals for several days or a week at a time saves time and preserves sanity. Think in terms of three-meal planning and include snacks. Having a menu plan eliminates boredom and allows for variety as well as for better nutrition for the family. Looking over a week's plans, you can see whether the essential foods have been included and perhaps make some changes here and there, adding more protective foods where needed. Also, plan for moderation. All foods have calories and excessive calories cause many health problems.

After you have planned weekly menus for awhile, it will become easier and you can plan for more than one week if you have adequate storage space. You will soon find that the time spent in this planning pays rich dividends.

Develop a Recipe Card File
Start a collection of quick, fat-free, health-conscious recipes. After a recipe passes the taste test, enter it in a card file or in a spiral notebook. Develop recipes that let you cook once and eat two or three times.

Prepare Ahead for No-Stress Cooking
Where would the busy cook be without the freezer? In the kitchen, of course, Make-ahead meals stored in the freezer are the unsung heroes of shortcut cooking. They just wait to be called into action, and make you look like you have slaved and fussed all day when all you've done is thawed and heated. Cook up double batches. Freeze one, and you get two meals with one preparation.

Some foods that freeze well are soups, sauces, casseroles, breads, cookies, and most meats. Do not freeze raw vegetables, foods with mayonnaise or cooked egg whites.

Meals in Minutes
A kitchen stocked with versatile ingredients adds sparkle to tasty dishes. These all-purpose items can be added at the last minute:

● Plain yogurt keeps well and is a healthy base for sauces and dressings. Add cheese, herbs or lemon juice for steamed vegetables. Whip it into omelets or use it to top baked potatoes.

● Shelled nuts add crunch and flavor to stir-fry dishes, fruit salads, tuna or chicken salad.

● No kitchen should ever be without cooked brown rice, bulgur, pasta or soup to add heartiness to simple meals. Slivered meat, turkey or chicken, or lots of fresh vegetables served over brown rice or pasta saves time and adds nutrition.

● Whole wheat spaghetti or macaroni served with a sauce containing small amounts of meat, chicken or fish and plenty of vegetables complemented by a green salad saves time and tempers.

● Keep a "salad bar" in the fridge—plastic bags or other containers of crisp greens washed and ready to mix with a selection of prepared crunchy veggies.

● Stock up on speedy add-ons and snappy flavor changers such as garlic, onion powder, curry, oregano, vegetable seasonings, honey, mustard, tamari and chili sauce.

Do Your Weekly Shopping All at Once

Compile one large grocery list and eliminate last minute panic. This will cut down on the number of trips to the grocery store. The more trips you take to the grocery store, and the longer time spent shopping, the more money you spend.

BE SUPERMARKET-WISE

It takes the willpower of a saint to walk through a modern supermarket and buy only according to your grocery list. But the challenge can be fun. The object of your trip to the supermarket is to choose between the

12,000 or so different items available for the tastiest, healthiest and most economical foods without wrecking your budget. It *is* possible to make wise food selections and avoid the built-in traps that lurk on every shelf.

Smart shoppers must be aware of supermarket danger zones, tempting food displays or the trap of impulse buying. Supermarket owners know that over 70 percent of all purchases will be "unplanned." How many times have you dashed to the store to pick up a loaf of bread or a carton of milk and come home with far more? These frequently needed items are generally at the back of the store as far from the entrance as possible. And many stores have special bargain displays or offer free samples of food. Do you have the willpower to pass up the free ice cream cone or pizza sample? Or do you walk out with the store special? Save your shape and your budget—avoid impulse buying.

A survival guide for supermarket know-how is a necessity for health conscious families. But your survival guide will not be effective unless you use it properly with you in control. Leave the supermarket with what you need, not what the advertisers want you to purchase. Get back to the basics. Remember that every processing step decreases nutrients and in-variably adds calories.

SURVIVAL GUIDE
FOR SMART SUPERMARKET SAVVY

1. Plan menus for a full week if possible. Make your menus realistic, based on seasonal items. Double-check your recipes against what you have on hand in order to avoid additional shopping trips which are

expensive, time consuming and encourage impulse buying.

2. Make a shopping list and keep it handy in the kitchen to list items needed. Shoppers without a list spend more time and money in the supermarket. Also, surveys show that when you are in the store over 20 minutes, you spend more money. Purchase only what you have on your list. Remember that high fat content snacks add 15 percent to your food bill and inches to your waistline.

3. Shop the areas of the store where the more nutritious foods are located such as the fresh fruits and vegetables.

4. Buy fresh fruits and vegetables in season since they cost less and are of better quality. One way to judge a supermarket is by the way the produce section looks—are the vegetables inviting and fresh-looking, or are they wilted, poorly trimmed or stacked in a haphazard manner? Avoid vegetables that have been watered and are dripping wet—they won't keep as well. Purchase only what you need unless you plan to freeze the extra right away.

When fresh fruits are not in season, purchase frozen or canned. Select the juice-pack or water-pack. If you must buy fruit in light syrup, rinse the "syrup" fruits with water before using. Never buy fruits packed in heavy syrup. Purchase unsweetened frozen fruits. It is usually more practical to purchase the larger size frozen bags of vegetables and fruits, even for small families, and cook only what you need. The quality and taste are "fresher" than those packed in the ten ounce size.

5. Do the refrigeration cases for dairy products, cheese and eggs appear adequate? Are the storage cartons and areas clean? Check the products for open dating which means the last day the product should be

sold. Look for low-fat, skim or partially skim products. For instance, plain yogurt costs less and is lower in fat and calories than fruit-on-the-bottom varieties. Purchase plain yogurt and add your own fruit. Reach for 1 or 2 percent low-fat cottage cheese.

6. Do not overbuy meat since protein is a costly item. Remember, you pay more per serving for pre-cut meat or poultry. Even if your family eats only white meat, purchase a whole chicken and use the dark meat in stews or casseroles. Take advantage of occasional store bargains such as turkey drumsticks which can be barbecued or stewed, the meat removed from the bone, diced, and used in tacos, enchiladas or pot pies.

7. Consider the cost of convenience foods. Sliced meats cost more than unsliced, for instance. Be a wise shopper and compare the costs of fresh raw, frozen, canned or dried foods in light of the time you have available for preparation and cooking.

Each serving of the following provides 20 grams of protein:

1 pound dry beans = 5 servings
1 pound raw, boneless lean meat = 4 servings
1 pound raw, fat and bony meat = 2 servings
1 pound canned beans = 2 servings

8. Look for 100 percent grains. Seek out unsweetened, whole grain granola, rolled oats, wheat bran, shredded wheat, brown rice, bulgur, cracked wheat, steel cut oats, popcorn, puffed wheat or rice. Choose those staples without artificial colors, flavors, or preservatives and with no added sugar. Day old bread saves money with little or no loss in nutritional value.

9. Be an informed and determined consumer. Let your supermarket manager know that you want more

low-fat, no-sugar and no-salt products if you do not find them. Praise him when you find these healthier alternatives available.

10. Read labels. Be a smart shopper. Learning to decipher the small print can be a healthy habit. All food labels must provide product name, manufacturer, packer, net weight or contents as well as the list of ingredients. Remember: first is most.

Check out the additives and colors listed. "Natural" foods generally contain fewer chemical additives than processed foods. The shorter the ingredient list, the more nutritional the product.

Check all nutritional information provided such as the number of calories per serving, grams of protein, carbohydrates, fat, and sodium. Some labels give cholesterol content and the source of the fats used in the product. Nutritional information can help you to be "naturally" selective.

Be aware that "sugarless" or "sugar-free" products do not contain white sugar, but may contain fructose, glucose, maltose, mannose, ribose, lactose, hexitol, mannitol, tylitol, sorbitol—all sweeteners with the same calories as white sugar. Learn to translate sugar content. One teaspoon equals four grams. If a product contains 12 grams of sucrose per serving, it equals three teaspoons of sugar per serving.

"Low-calorie" or "reduced calorie" products must contain no more than 40 calories per serving. Canned fruits must state the kind of liquid they contain. "No-added" salt on a label may mean that sodium-rich sources were used in the preparation.

11. Check the generic brands. The "no frills" generic brands are usually packaged under the store's name and may contain fewer additives and preservatives than regular brands. Store brands of paper products,

beauty aids or household cleaners are generally of the same quality as nationally advertised brands. Compare prices and quality, however, when buying generics. You may find that some are great buys and others may prove disappointing.

12. Volume purchasing may be wise for large families, particularly if you shop at a warehouse that sells by the case with no fancy displays and where you are expected to "bag your own." Surveys have shown that discount stores offer a savings of 20 to 35 percent over regular supermarket prices.

13. Watch the ads for comparative prices and seasonal specials. When you pay for your groceries at the check-out counter, check to be sure the clerk rings up the sale price rather than the regular one.

14. Coupon clipping can be time consuming but coupons that you actually need can save you money. If you don't need the item or have to buy three packages when you use only one package a year, then the coupons don't make much sense. Evaluate the time you spend on cutting, tearing, filing and organizing and weigh it against your actual savings.

15. After you shop, try to get home as soon as possible to store foods properly. Refrigerate meats, dairy products, fruits, eggs and vegetables promptly in order to preserve their nutrients. Don't wash fruits or vegetables before putting them in the refrigerator. Store in the crisper or in an air-tight container.

Food is one of God's gifts to us and we are admonished to be good stewards of His bounty. *"He who is generous will be blessed for he gives some of his food to the poor"* (Proverbs 22:9, NASB). And in Matthew 25:40 Jesus said that to share His bounty is like giving it to Him (Matthew 25:40).

Check to see if you are wasting food by serving your family too much. Encourage the practice of "take only what you will eat." Examine what practical changes can be made to save you money and to share with those who are hungry. *"As we have therefore opportunity, let us do good unto all men, especially unto them who are of the household of faith"* (Galatians 6:10).

3
Healthy Beginnings for Super Babies

Jesus loved little children. He said, *"Suffer little children to come unto me and forbid them not: for of such is the kingdom of God"* (Luke 18:16). Jesus wanted all children to be loved and to be taught to follow His laws. If the Lord Jesus loves children that much, our children and grandchildren deserve the very best that we can give them.

No loving parent would deliberately hinder a little one from becoming the healthy, vibrant, positive person our Creator intended. Yet every time we serve fake, non-nutritious foods, we fill little bodies with foreign chemicals that should not be there.

Remind yourself "that ye are the temple of God, and the Spirit of God dwelleth in you" (I Corinthians 3:16-17).

Life took on a heavenly glow known only to grand-mothers when my daughter, Judi, presented me with identical twin granddaughters in 1980. What a blessing they are to everyone who meets them and how they fill our lives with beauty and happiness.

Joanna and Claire weighed at full-term birth, 6 pounds 10 ounces and 6 pounds 14 ounces respectively—quite a hefty bundle for a petite mom who is five feet and normally weighs 106 pounds! Judi's pediatrician informed us that the babies were the only ones not jaundiced in the nursery.

These two very special little people have been an endless source of wonder and delight for me while broadening my education considerably—notwithstanding the knowledge I had accumulated while feeding and teaching 109 million school kids throughout the years.

Too many children are born into this world with birth defects, respiratory distress, rickets, drug addiction, low birth weight, brain damage and numerous other problems. Young adults, as potential parents, should visit the premature nursery in any hospital for a sobering lesson in the importance of taking care of their bodies prior to and during pregnancy.

In the '60's Americans talked about finding themselves. In the '70's they talked about careers and making money. Today the Yuppies (baby boomers of the World War II era) talk about babies and have brought Motherhood back in style.

This new crop of mothers are more realistic and know that their true fulfillment must include parenting. The parents of the '80's are better prepared, which would please Dr. John Myers who wrote in *Metabolic Aspects of Health* that if all women would prepare for pregnancy in the same way the soil of a garden is prepared with trace elements and organic fertilizers *before* the seed is planted, all children would have a better start in life.

Who are today's new mothers? A large percentage of the women entering motherhood are those we used to think of as older—thirty-four or thirty-five years of age. Judi was thirty-four years old when blessed with the birth of twins. She and father-to-be, Jerry, prepared themselves well and did not miss out on any of the breathtaking moments of the experience. Theirs was an attitude of "*we're* pregnant."

Together they attended pre-natal classes where they met other prospective parents and exchanged experiences and shared ideas. I want to share with you Judi's "Before and After Health Plan."

JUDI'S BEFORE
AND AFTER HEALTH PLAN

Bonding

Pregnancy should be a love affair between Mom, Dad and baby as soon as talk about having a baby begins. The love affair intensifies as conception takes place and when the first movements are felt.

The mother communicates her feelings, thoughts and activities as well as what she eats to the unborn baby. So many of us do not realize that in the pre-natal environment, baby is already listening. That mysterious process that goes on between parent and child is called "bonding." I did not realize how important the pre-natal forces are until my daughter's pregnancy. The psychic influence of the mother on the baby during pregnancy is extremely important.

The evidence shows that fetuses hear. They hear what the mother says, and what she says affects them. The fetus listens to the comforting sounds of the mother's heartbeat and the digestive gurgles, but some outside noises also penetrate. Babies definitely prefer the sound of the mother's voice above all others. Dad's voice doesn't seem to penetrate the womb as well—maybe because the mother's voice has a direct linkage to the baby.

Dr. Thomas Verny in his book, *The Secret Life of the Unborn Child*, states that unborn children are responsive to light, music, maternal eating, sleeping, marital stress and deliberate attempts of parents to communicate with them. (This grandma was not going to be left out and enjoyed talking to her unborn grandchildren.)

Dr. Verny stated also that at 16 weeks a fetus is startled by a beam of light flashed on the mother. The six month fetus can see, hear, feel, taste, remember, learn, experience emotion and show distinct musical preferences. For instance, Dr. Verny found that Mozart and Vivaldi are calming, while Brahms, Beethoven and all forms of rock music cause violent kicking.

So if you find that singing softly or talking directly to your unborn child brings you pleasure, feel free to enjoy yourself. Parent-child bonding begins in the womb and birth is a continuation of a dialogue begun earlier.

Correct Breathing and Oxygen

Oxygen is an important nutrient to baby. Learning to breathe slowly and deeply is vital for preparing Mom for the stresses of labor and to keep the flow of life-giving oxygen constant to baby. Never hold your breath, even when exercising, since this cuts off the supply of oxygen to the baby. Nicotine in cigarettes is a powerful constrictor of blood vessels which reduces the amount of oxygen the baby receives. Pregnant women who smoke have an increased risk of a miscarriage or a stillborn baby. Babies of mothers who smoke are smaller than normal at birth. Tobacco smoke also triggers allergies, asthma and ear problems in children. It takes the fetus 1½ hours to recover from one cigarette smoked by the mother.

Fresh Air, Sunlight and Pure Water

Low-stress living in a semi-country atmosphere with very little pollution contributed to Judi's healthful environment. Plenty of sunshine and fresh air not only increased nutrient absorption but were stress-reducers as well. Their pure well water provided a welcome thirst quencher and plenty of fluids for Mom.

Water is second only to oxygen as a prerequisite for life. Drinking adequate amounts of water helps the body rid itself of sodium which contributes to water retention. During pregnancy lots of fluids are needed to support expanding blood volume and baby's growth.

Sleep and Rest

Few habits have a more direct relationship to how Mom feels and looks than her sleep habits. Sleepless nights cause fatigue lines in the face as well as puffiness around the eyes. Sleep is important for mental and physical well-being as well as the cosmetic benefits of making us look more youthful.

In Judi's case her abdomen became so large in the later stages of pregnancy that sleep was uncomfortable. She found that sleeping on her side with a pillow propped between her knees gave the abdomen more space and took the pressure off the pelvic area. Short day-time naps with the feet and legs elevated also helped her relax and renew her energy.

Most mothers and fathers find the first few weeks with a new baby uniquely rewarding, challenging—and extremely exhausting. Preserve your energies by taking it slowly and nap as much as possible when baby does.

To achieve more relaxed sleep:

1. Countdown to sleep. Make sure that your system is not on overdrive following the evening meal. Begin to taper off all mental activity. Fresh air and gentle exercise help to unwind.

2. Keep it light. Dine early and remember that calories consumed after 8:00 p.m. go to make more body fat. A calcium-spiked snack of yogurt, cheese or milk may help at bedtime. Milk also contains high levels of an amino acid, tryptophan, which helps to induce sleep.

3. Avoid chemical stimulants. Caffeine speeds up the metabolism and may cause wakefulness for up to seven hours.

4. Don't watch stimulating television programs or get involved in thought-provoking discussions just before bedtime. Read a good book instead, or listen to soothing music.

5. Take a warm bath before going to bed. Try to relax and soothe those muscles.

6. Learn to make your "body clock" work for you. Regular bedtime patterns (easier to adjust to *before* baby comes) are sleep-inducers.

Exercise

Those moms who were in top physical shape "before" should not abandon their exercise routine during pregnancy. When the pelvic muscles are strong and flexible, there are not as many problems during pregnancy and birth. Aerobic exercise strengthens heart and lung efficiency, muscular flexibility, one's self-image and stamina, as well as helping the body work off stress, worry and body toxins while delivering nutrients more thoroughly throughout the body.

Sluggish pelvic muscles cannot firmly support the increasing weight of pregnancy. Inactivity causes muscular discomfort, added fat, constipation and digestive disorders, depression and poor emotional health.

Childbirth in itself is extremely physical and an enjoyable, productive experience in the delivery and recovery rooms may depend on the mother's fitness level.

Exercise after pregnancy can be beneficial, too, in eliminating post-partum depression. Exercise helps defeat depression by getting oxygen into the lungs and getting the blood moving.

Remember these things about exercise during pregnancy, however:

● Check with your doctor or obstetrician before undertaking an exercise program.

● Don't make any drastic changes in your routine. Continue what exercise you were doing before pregnancy.

● Stay away from horseback riding, strenuous tennis or motorcycle riding.

● Sitting can be a major cause of backache. Take the strain off the back by sitting upright and cross-legged with the bottom of the feet together. Use a pillow on the floor for maximum benefit.

Weight Gain

Too much emphasis is placed on how much weight an expectant mother should gain and not enough attention is given to what nutrients are being eaten. Babies are more likely to suffer when too much attention is devoted to controlling mother's weight, rather than mom's nutrition.

The last two months of pregnancy are extremely important for the normal baby's growth spurts. This development can be seriously hindered when the mother has reached the weight gain prescribed by her doctor and begins to curtail her eating patterns. She may actually starve her baby. Weight restriction generally results in smaller babies. Babies below a birth weight of five and a half pounds have greater risk for health problems.

Two major factors determine the baby's birth weight: the height and weight of the mother before conception and the amount of weight gained during pregnancy.

The baby has to depend on what the mother eats for its growth and development. Poor nutrition in early pregnancy affects baby's development and ability to survive. The best nourished babies are those whose mothers have always had healthy eating habits. An underweight woman who gains weight during pregnancy may be diverting nutrients her baby needs in order to replenish her own deficiencies.

The amount of weight the mother gains is important in determining baby's birth weight. Years ago weight gain was limited to 20 pounds and many of us dreaded that check-in with the scales. Now we know that it takes around 80,000 calories just to make a baby and this does not include the needs of the mother. This adds up to a weight gain of 24 to 30 pounds and more for twins.

Weight should be gained at a slow and steady rate, not in sudden spurts since baby needs a continuous supply of nutrients. Usually a weight gain of three to four pounds in the first three months is normal (provided it is not a multiple birth) and around four pounds per month after that. The last three months is the time of the most rapid brain development for baby when the need for calories and protein is critical. Throughout a pregnancy 75 to 100 grams of protein a day is recommended depending on the mother's body size, weight and activity level.

If calories are severely restricted toward the end of pregnancy, the baby's development may be seriously hampered.

Judi gained 50 pounds during her pregnancy and one year later was only ten pounds heavier than her pre-pregnancy weight thanks to healthful eating and exercise. Her doctor did not limit salt and encouraged her to consume additional calories and more quality proteins since she was eating for three. Her twins were carried full term with normal birth weights.

Role of Nutrition

Building a healthy baby does not give Mom the right to eat everything in sight, however, even if she is eating for three. When the mother's goal is to give birth to the healthiest baby possible, she refuses to take chances with her diet. What are the healthiest foods for pregnancy? The same basic, whole foods that provide nutrients for optimum health when non-pregnant. Pregnancy requires increasing many nutrients, including a wide variety of all foods, since you're building a new human being. Remember, in pregnancy there is no "instant replay," so make your game plan work the first time.

NUTRIENTS IMPORTANT FOR MOTHERS-TO-BE

When eating for two (or three as in Judi's case), be sure to include in your feeding plan the following important nutrients:

Protein

Protein builds baby's body cells and provides for rapid mental and physical development. Growth retardation or mental deprivation can result from inadequate protein. Maternal tissue, blood volume, as well as energy needs during delivery are met with adequate protein. Increase your daily level up to 75 or 100 grams based on individual body needs.

Use the attached chart to help you reach your protein requirements.

Sources of Proteins

PROTEIN FOODS	AMOUNT	GRAMS OF PROTEIN
Almonds	½ cup	15
Bagel	1	6
Baked potato	1 medium	5
Beef	3½ ounces	20-30
Beef, dried	3 ounces	30
Buckwheat	½ cup	10
Cheese, Swiss, cheddar or muenster	2 ounces	20
Chicken	4 ounces	20-30
Cottage cheese	½ cup	20-25
Egg, fresh	1 large	8
Fish, broiled/lean	4 ounces	20-30
Gelatin, plain	1 tablespoon	8
Hamburger, lean	3 ounces	20
Lamb chops	2 small	20
Lentils	½ cup	10
Lima beans	½ cup	5
Liver, all kinds	4 ounces	20-25
Milk, dry/skim	½ cup	22
Milk, whole	1 quart	34
Mushrooms	½ cup	8
Navy beans	½ cup	6

Oatmeal	1 cup	5
Peanuts	½ cup	20
Peanut butter	½ cup	24
Peas, dried	½ cup	20
Pecans	½ cup	5
Rice, brown	½ cup	8
Salmon	3 ounces	22
Seeds (sunflower, sesame, pumpkin, squash)	½ cup	20-24
Shrimp	10 medium	12
Soya flour	½ cup	35
Soybeans	½ cup	37
Steak	4 ounces	20
Tofu	4 ounces	10
Tuna fish	3 ounces	15
Turkey	4 ounces	23
Waffle (enriched)	1	7
Walnuts	½ cup	10
Wheat germ, fresh	3½ ounces	26.6
Whole grain bread	1 slice	3
Yogurt	1 cup	8½

Complex Carbohydrates

For energy and fuel, be sure to include at least 55 to 60 percent of your calories in complex carbohydrates such as whole grain breads and cereals, pasta, brown rice, millet, cracked wheat, corn, potatoes, fruits and vegetables. Eat four or more servings of these vitality boosters every day.

Calcium

Calcium is the body's most abundant mineral and without it there would be:
NO beating heart
NO muscles and nerves
NO blood clotting

65

NO strong teeth
NO healthy, firm bones

Pregnancy and breast feeding put a drain on calcium reserves, so be certain that you increase calcium by at least 50 percent (approximately 1500 to 1800 milligrams a day) based upon individual needs.

When the mother's diet is deficient in calcium, the body dips into the calcium reserves, such as the mother's bones. This weakens them and results in inadequate amounts for baby's teeth, bones and cell development. Milk and dairy products are the best sources of calcium with 1 cup of milk supplying 291 milligrams of calcium. (Buttermilk is as rich as whole milk in calcium.) Do not add chocolate to milk since chocolate is high in fat and contains theobromine which reduces the body's absorption of calcium.

Other sources of calcium equivalents include green leafy vegetables (collards being the richest in calcium), barley, almonds, sardines, salmon, sesame seeds and tofu.

Sources of Calcium

FOOD	AMOUNT	CALCIUM
Almonds, raw	8 ounces	332 milligrams
Cheese, Cheddar, Swiss, etc.	2 ounces	408 milligrams
Collards, cooked	4 ounces	179 milligrams
Dried buttermilk	8 ounces	1,421 milligrams
Evaporated milk sweetened, not reconstituted	8 ounces	802 milligrams
Evaporated milk unsweetened, not reconstituted	8 ounces	635 milligrams

Goat's milk	8 ounces	315 milligrams
Kale, cooked	4 ounces	103 milligrams
Milk, skim	8 ounces	297 milligrams
Milk, whole	8 ounces	291 milligrams
Non-fat dry milk	8 ounces	302 milligrams
Non-fat instant milk	8 ounces	837 milligrams
Ricotta cheese (whole milk)	1 ounce	509 milligrams
Salmon, drained	4 ounces	365 milligrams
Sardines drained, solids	4 ounces	494 milligrams
Sesame seeds	2 tablespoons	210 milligrams
Tofu	4 ounces	150 milligrams
Turnip greens, cooked	4 ounces	134 milligrams
Watercress	8 ounces	189 milligrams
Yogurt, plain	8 ounces	415 milligrams

Calcium Robbers

1. Lack of exercise. Bones need stress to stay healthy.

2. A high protein diet results in too much phosphorus. This interferes with the body's ability to absorb calcium. Beware! Soft drinks are extremely high in phosphorus which is added to keep them from becoming cloudy. Carbonated soft drinks deplete the body's calcium reserve. Phosphorus should NEVER EXCEED calcium intake.

3. Caffeine. Two cups of coffee causes a loss of 22 milligrams of calcium.

4. Drugs, antibiotics and smoking.

5. Excessive sugar increases the rate at which calcium is excreted.

Calcium Enhancers

1. Keep a calcium diary to be sure you consume enough.

2. Increase daily exercise to enhance bone formation.

3. Soups are "souper" sources of calcium. Make soup the old-fashioned way using lots of bones and vegetables.

4. Get enough sunlight. This triggers the production of vitamin D required for absorbing calcium. (The need for vitamin D doubles during pregnancy. Vitamin D is obtained from direct sunlight, fortified milk, egg yolks, liver, sardines, canned salmon and butter.)

5. Vitamin C foods enhance the absorption of calcium.

6. Substitute grated cheese or parmesan instead of butter on vegetables.

7. When making a salad, use the darker, deeper greens and remember that the darker the greens, the more nutrients. Garnish your salad with fresh kale or parsley. EAT the garnish.

8. To boost calcium and protein quality, enjoy Hi-Vitality Milk.

To make Hi-Vitality milk, put one cup of dry skim milk into a quart of fresh milk (skim milk if you are watching your weight). This tastes like real milk or cream. Within this one quart of milk, you have the nourishment of two quarts—70 grams of good protein, rich in calcium and the beautifying B vitamins. Drink this basic, lean Hi-Vi milk. Use it with cereals, in cooking, and keep a bottle of it in your refrigerator at all times. Before retiring at night, check up on your protein and calcium intake and make up any deficiency with this high vitality milk.

Iron

Iron is crucial during pregnancy and is essential for the formation of red blood cells. The mother's need for the volume of blood increases and the baby takes from the mother regardless of her supply. The baby stores up iron for his first few months following birth. Without adequate iron, mothers become exhausted, anemic and more susceptible to infection.

Very few women start pregnancy with enough iron. Iron supplements are usually recommended by the doctor throughout pregnancy and for several months afterwards. Since vitamin C helps iron absorption, eat something containing ascorbic acid (vitamin C) with iron-rich foods. Putting tomatoes on a hamburger helps as well as eating a serving of oranges, grapefruits or strawberries along with your meal.

It's "iron-ic" that liver and spinach—two of the most disliked foods—are also two of the most iron-rich. For non-liver lovers, grind liver and cook with ground beef. Use in recipes containing tomatoes or tomato sauce to help disguise the taste.

Rich Sources of Iron

Liver	Dark leafy vegetables
Fried beans	Fresh and dried apricots
Oysters	Raisins
Beets	Barley
Parsley	Bananas
Prunes	Molasses

Iron Antagonists

Boiling vegetables in water leaches as much as 20 percent of the iron. Steam cook vegetables or save the cooking water to use in broths and soups. Cook in cast-iron utensils for better iron absorption.

Supplements of calcium, zinc and manganese in high dosages depress iron absorption.

Antacids, especially those containing calcium carbonate, decrease iron.

Sulphur compounds and toxic metals (particularly lead) impair iron utilization.

High intake of coffee or tea interferes with iron absorption.

Folic Acid

Folic acid is necessary for cell division and the need for it doubles during pregnancy. A deficiency of folic acid or folacin can result in sudden abortion or damage to the fetus. Foods rich in folic acid include liver, leafy dark green vegetables, whole grains and blackstrap molasses.

Fat Soluble Vitamins

These are vitamins A, D, E and F. They must first dissolve in fat before being absorbed by the body. During pregnancy an increase of at least 25 percent is required for vitamins A and E. Both of these vitamins act as antioxidants protecting cells and membranes. Include generous amounts of dark green leafy vegetables, cabbage, broccoli, parsley, deep yellow or orange fruits and vegetables, liver, seafood, butter, golden vegetable oils, fish and fish oils, whole grains and wheat germ.

Water Soluble Vitamins

All of the B complex vitamins and vitamin C are dissolved in water. These vitamins are *not* stored in the body and are needed daily. Vitamin B_6 may be needed in larger amounts during pregnancy, particularly by those mothers who were previously on the birth control pill. The amounts of B_6 should be prescribed by your doctor. Foods rich in the B complex vitamins include brewers yeast, liver, whole grains, spinach, bananas, nuts, potatoes, leafy green vegetables and meats.

Vitamin C is also known as ascorbic acid and the need for this protective vitamin increases during pregnancy to keep the uterus strong. Vitamin C protects all other vitamins and is extremely sensitive to light, air, heat and water. So don't cut up fruit or tomatoes in advance and leave them setting on the kitchen counter. Overwashing and overcutting fruits and vegetables also depletes vitamin C.

Foods rich in vitamin C include all citrus fruits, cantaloupes, peaches, strawberries, papayas, root vegetables, leafy green vegetables, berries, sprouts, tomatoes, potatoes, red and green peppers (red contains more than green), broccoli and all cabbage family vegetables.

Be sure to eat the white skin under the peeling of oranges or grapefruit since this is where the bioflavonoids are located. The bioflavonoids protect vitamin C and keep blood vessels and capillaries strong. Doctors usually increase the amount of vitamin C during pregnancy by at least one third or more. The amount prescribed may range from 100 milligrams to 1000 milligrams a day.

Cigarette smoking or even breathing cigarette smoke destroys vitamin C. Approximately 25 milligrams are destroyed for each cigarette consumed. Pregnant women should be very careful. Smoking can be extremely harmful to the development of a fetus.

Minerals

Magnesium, potassium and zinc need to be included in the mother's eating plan to insure development of baby's bones, nerves, muscles, heart vessels, cellular balance, hormones, energy production and tissue growth. Healthy amounts of these nutrients are generally consumed when eating a balanced variety of super foods such as broccoli, bran, bananas, wheat germ, yogurt, carrots, cantaloupes, collard greens, tomatoes, tofu, salad greens, parsley, sunflower seeds, pumpkin seeds, oranges, grapefruit, cucumbers, barley, sweet potatoes, mushrooms, potatoes (with skin), squash, dandelion greens (also high in vitamin C), seafood, pineapple, cabbage and onions.

For a super potassium-mineral broth:
Chop ½ cup of each of the following vegetables: carrots, potatoes (with peel), celery leaves, green pepper, cabbage and parsley. Add garlic clove and/or green onions with tops. Simmer until barely tender in a quart of water.

Season lightly with vegetable salt. Place in blender, whirl until you have a nicely thickened broth.

V-8 or tomato juice can be added for flavor. Zucchini, string beans, and okra can be used for variety. Drink warm or cold.

Additional zinc is also needed during pregnancy—almost a 50 percent increase. Foods rich in zinc are: seafood, chicken, fish, eggs, yogurt, non-fat dry milk, mushrooms, whole grains, pumpkin seeds, bran, peas, rolled oats, liver, and egg yolk.

All of the above nutrients can be combined into a flexible daily eating plan for two:

● Four or more servings of a high protein food such as meat, fish, poultry, eggs, cheese or vegetables to equal 15 to 20 grams of protein.

● Four servings of milk or its equivalent.

● Four to six servings of a combination of citrus fruits or vegetables rich in vitamin C, leafy green vegetables, potatoes and deep orange or yellow vegetables.

● Four to five servings of whole grain products including cereals, bread, pancakes, muffins and pasta.

● One to two tablespoons of fish oils or vegetable oils for essential fatty acids.

● Six or more glasses of water or juice in addition to milk for necessary fluids.

● Snacks keep energy levels constant. Enjoy raw vegetable slices, fresh fruit, sunflower seeds, toasted soy nuts, popcorn, unsweetened cereal crunch, parfaits, puddings, frozen ices, fruit-nut breads, whole grain crackers, cheese, tofu, bits of fish, turkey cubes, sardines, crackers and eggs.

What about vitamin supplements? Some doctors believe that a balanced diet of nourishing, healthy foods provides sufficient nutrients. Other doctors prescribe vitamin and mineral supplements before, during and following pregnancy based on individual needs. It's still important to "eat" your vitamins, though, not just take them in pill form. Vitamin supplements cannot replace food but they can help to insure against deficiencies. When prescribed, they should always be taken at mealtime.

JUDI'S NUTRITION PLAN

● Breakfast: Oatmeal with fresh fruit and whole grain toast varied with egg omelets.

● Lunch and dinner: Lean meat, chicken, turkey, plenty of fresh fish and seafood, liver, cottage cheese, yogurt, brown rice, wheatberries, fresh fruits and vegetables, nuts, seeds, eggs and milk. Judi did not limit her salt, took no medication, and has never had the "caffeine habit."

● Morning or mid-afternoon: Judi drank *Mom's Pep-up Drink* depending on her energy level or the activities of the day. To make this drink place the following ingredients in a blender:

> 1 cup of milk or unsweetened fresh juice
> (Whole milk, skim milk or low-fat milk can be used based on whether you're calorie-loading or calorie-reducing.)
> 2 teaspoons fresh wheat germ
> 2 to 3 tablespoons of protein powder
> (Made from eggs, milk and papaya; containing no sugar, artificial colorings, flavorings or preservatives. Be sure to check out the kind and amount of fat on the label.)
> ½ teaspoon vitamin C powder
> ¼ cup plain yogurt
> ½ banana or 3 to 5 fresh or frozen strawberries or peaches
> (More milk, juice or water may be needed if drink is too thick)

Blend all ingredients together until smooth and store in the refrigerator. Drink whenever a boost is needed.

Judi continues to use the *Pep-up* drink as a meal on the run, a beauty booster or to help ease her through the "arsenic hour frenzies" which occur for Mom and toddlers around five o'clock in the afternoon. (Grandma also enjoys the *Pep-up* drink as a vitality booster.)

NURSING AND STARTING SOLID FOODS

Judi nursed both babies from birth, surprising even her pediatrician. He had had only one other mother in 30 years successfully nurse twins. Nursing not only provides bonding, cuddling, warmth, security, love, rest, fewer allergies, less fat cells, increased immunity and food but is convenient, available and economical as well. It even helps Mom to regain her figure.

When breast feeding, a mother should add an additional 500 calories a day to her diet and maintain nutritional requirements similar to pregnancy, including plenty of quality protein, calcium-rich foods such as milk, yogurt, cheese, tofu, sesame seeds, dark green leafy vegetables as well as eggs, lean meats, fresh fruits, and whole grains. (Mom's *Pep-up Drink* is excellent for nursing mothers, too.) Liquids should be increased to around three quarts a day in the form of milk or yogurt (four to six cups), water, fruit and vegetable juices.

A breast fed baby may require as much as $5,000 less in dental care during a lifetime. Breast feeding results in :

- helping the jaw to develop properly.
- less need for orthodontics.
- less tooth decay.
- less periodontal disease.
- less myofunctional problems.
- better absorption of nutrients to protect against low-calcium levels.
- iron is more easily available and absorbed.
- the presence of arachidonic acid enhances brain development.
- lower levels of sodium (much less than in formula milk).
- high levels of lactoferrin which inhibits harmful bacteria in the intestines.

I have been privileged to be on three worldwide programs in the La Leche League International and am always impressed by the healthy children and the caring mothers and fathers. Their material on breast feeding is excellent and is available by writing to La Leche League International, P.O. Box 1209, Franklin Park, Illinois 60131-8209.

Mother's touch is almost as nourishing for baby as her milk. Close bodily contact is very important in the first few months of a baby's life. This touch-growth connection produces babies who smile more and cry less even when left alone. Infants who do not have this close bodily contact and caressing do not grow as well.

Dr. Lewis A. Coffin in his book *Children's Nutrition* states that in his experience as a pediatrician "brief skin to skin contact between mother and newly born infant within the first hour or so after birth seems to confer increased resistance to infection upon the child. Blood sugar often drops precipitously after delivery, all too often in the nursery where it may not be suspected or treated. If a newborn baby is put to breast shortly after birth (in such a way as to protect against dangerous cooling) the advantage of this increased resistance to infection is gained and hypoglycemia is averted." (From *Children's Nutrition* by Lewis A. Coffin, M.D., 1984, Capra Press, P.O. Box 2068, Santa Barbara, CA 93120.)

In 1983 the American Academy of Pediatric's Committee on Nutrition issued the following recommendations regarding the feeding of little ones:

(1) Dietary fat and cholesterol should not be limited during the first year.

(2) Breast feeding is preferred, but when not possible, commercial infant formulas are the best alternative for the first year. Skim milk should not be given. Solid foods may be introduced at four to six months.

(3) After one year of age a varied diet from each of the major food groups is the best assurance of nutritional adequacy.

(4) Infants and children should be weighed and measured regularly to permit early recognition of obesity. Maintenance of ideal body weight and a regular exercise program is important.

(5) A family history of premature heart attacks or strokes (at age 60 or less), hypertension, obesity and hyperlipidemia indicates those children should be screened at age two.

Based on all of the information available, how does the nutrition-wise mom go about introducing solid foods to baby? Each child is unique, responding in his or her own way to different feeding programs. Each mother, with the advice of her pediatrician, must work out the program best suited for her child.

Necessary equipment for a new mother includes a

blender or food processor, food mill, baby grinder, and non-stick cooking utensils.

Generally solid foods are not started until...
● Baby is able to sit well, can swallow and has good control of its neck and head. (The extrusion reflex does not disappear until nearly four months of age. The neuromuscular coordination necessary for swallowing solid foods is not fully developed until four or four and a half months of age.)
● Baby is able to lean forward to grab the spoon or turn his or her head away to indicate fullness.

Judi was fortunate in being able to nurse Joanna and Claire until nearly six months of age. Her pediatrician labeled the twins as "disgustingly healthy." When it came time to introduce them to solid food, Judi prepared it fresh herself. Some of her secrets for successfully introducing solid foods included...

● Keep the association with food a pleasant, relaxed experience. Feeding baby should be planned when the mother or father are not rushed.
● Keep your facial expression happy and smiling. Babies can sense tension, irritability or impatience.
● Introduce only one new food at a time and wait at least five or six days before trying another new food. Combining too many foods too soon causes digestive upsets or future food allergies.
● Use eating utensils designed for infants, particularly a very small spoon and cup. Feed baby slowly and in very small amounts to give baby time to swallow.
● Do not try to overfeed. When baby gets restless or turns away, stop feeding right away. Forcing baby to eat too much may create a tendency to future obesity.

● Introduce the new solid food first before offering the breast or bottle to baby.

Remember, "Pleasant words are as a honeycomb, sweet to the soul, and health to the bones" (Proverbs 16:24).

Brown rice cream cereal mixed with a little goat's milk was the first solid food introduced to Joanna and Claire. After several weeks on the brown rice cereal, fruits were introduced one at a time at weekly intervals. Seasonal fresh fruits included bananas, apples, applesauce, peaches, apricots, pears and avocados—all strained and pureed, scraped, blended or liquified. No sugar or salt was added. (The brown rice cream cereal was obtained from Walnut Acres, Penns Creek, Pennsylvania 17862. Their free catalogue is filled with organically grown, nutritious foods. The 12 grain cereal, oatmeal, maple-almond granola, sunburst banana breakfast, millet, pancake mixes, banana-date peanut butter and brown rice are super. Watch out. These foods are so delicious, they become addictive—especially the banana peanut butter.)

Later the babies enjoyed coddled eggs mixed with the cereal and Judi obtained fresh eggs from a neighbor on a farm nearby. A favorite egg omelet which they still enjoy contains approximately 32 grams of protein. Here's the recipe.

Beat 2 eggs and place in a non-stick skillet. Cook lightly until eggs are ready to fold, then add ⅓ cup of cottage cheese, blend together and serve at once. For "quick starters," beat the eggs and cottage cheese together and "scramble," stirring constantly to keep from sticking. Variations of cheeses can include cream cheese (which the twins like), ricotta or tofu. (The egg omelet recipe is one of my favorites for "Grandmas on the Go." Exceptions—I substitute 1 whole egg with 2 egg whites and 1% uncreamed cottage cheese or tofu.)

Strained vegetables followed the introduction of fruits and eggs and were usually the same as those served at the family meal using no seasonings of any kind. Seeing them eat and enjoy vegetables has been rewarding. They actually like vegetables—all kinds. While other little ones gummed on french fries from the nearest golden arches, these two enjoyed baked potatoes (sometimes stuffed with yogurt, cottage cheese and brocooli), fresh squash, sweet potatoes, broccoli, carrots, peas and green beans. Little ones adore "fingering" peas and beans.

Protein foods added at 10 to 12 months consisted of cottage cheese, tofu, lean meat, tuna, salmon, chicken, turkey, liver (once a week), lentils, dry beans and fresh fish. Their dad kept the family supplied with fresh fish. He deboned and flaked white fish for Joanna and Claire. Mini portions of fish are kept in constant supply in the freezer—which also provides a perfect excuse for "going fishing."

Peanut butter mixed with one of the following is a big favorite with the girls: applesauce, dates, bananas, grated carrots, or pulverized raisins or sesame seeds.

Today the four-year-olds enjoy...

> Soups of all kinds (fish stew, chicken and rice, vegetable)
> Sandwiches (pita bread, English muffins, whole grain bread)

Pizza
Spaghetti
Meatloaf
Vegetable kabobs
Pancakes or waffles—topped with fresh or
    frozen fruit
French toast
Bean burgers
Melons
Stuffed celery
Puddings
Strawberries—Claire's favorite fruit
Blueberries and fresh pineapple—Joanna's
    favorite fruits
Fresh tomatoes—Claire's (Joanna will only eat
    fresh cherry tomatoes—when she picks
    them in Grandma's garden)

Cereal
Their mom has done a super job of explaining the sugared cereal commercials on television to the girls. How many young children do you know who select shredded wheat as their favorite? There are no highly sugared cereals in Judi's pantry. She varies cooked cereals with ready-to-eat cereals.

Walnut Acres' Sunburst Banana Breakfast contains cracked sunflower and pumpkin seeds, toasted wheat germ, skim milk powder, ground almonds, filberts, date pieces, toasted sesame seeds and chopped apples. This is delicious sprinkled on baked apples, yogurt or as a topping for fruit. Sometimes Judi places breakfast in a cup for snacking.

The Journal of Dentistry for Children recommends no more than 3 grams of sugar per 1 ounce serving. In the commercial cereal field, the cereals that meet these recommendations are:

Puffed Wheat or Millet	Wheaties
Puffed Rice	Wheat, Corn or Rice Chex
Shredded Wheat	Rice Krispies
(biscuit and bite-size	Grape Nut Flakes
without sugar)	Special K
Cheerios	Nutri-Grain (no raisins)

Health and Safety Guidelines
when preparing baby's food at home

1. When fresh food is not available, use frozen foods. Be sure that the fresh foods are in top condition so as to provide maximum nutrition.

2. Read baby food labels carefully when purchasing ready-prepared fruits, vegetables, juices or meats. There should be no added sugar, salt, fat, colorings or additives.

3. To preserve nutrients, vegetables should be steamed or pressure-cooked using as little water as possible.

4. Do not reheat leftovers for baby. Keep all foods tightly covered. Do not allow foods to remain uncovered or unrefrigerated.

5. Vegetables may be prepared and pureed, then poured into an ice cube tray and frozen. When completely frozen, remove the food from the tray, place in a sterilized freezer container, label and store in the freezer for several weeks.

DAILY TODDLER FOOD GUIDE

Milk or equivalent—2 cups

Protein Foods—2 to 3 servings to equal about 23 grams of protein a day
● Meat, chicken or turkey—a 2-inch square and ¼ inch thick
● ¼ cup cottage cheese
● 1 medium egg
● 2 tablespoons peanut butter or other nut butters
● ½ cup dry beans or peas
● 1 slice cheese
● 3 ounces tofu

Vegetables and Fruits—4 or more servings
● 2 to 3 tablespoons of vegetables
● ½ cup fresh fruit or ¼ cup cooked or canned fruit
Include vitamin C rich foods, vitamin A rich foods, potatoes and other fruits and vegetables.

Bread and Cereals—3 to 4 servings
This includes ½ slice whole grain bread, ¼ cup cooked cereal, pasta or brown rice or ⅓ cup dry cereal.

Frankfurters are not recommended for children under three years of age due to their inability to chew thoroughly and the danger of choking. Nitrite-free frankfurters are the best nutritional choice. Chicken or turkey frankfurters are acceptable alternatives. Always serve a vitamin C fruit or juice when consuming frankfurters containing nitrites or nitrates to counteract the nitrosamines which may cause cancer.

Chewing gum containing aspartame or xylitol may cause stomach cramps or diarrhea in children.

Most pediatricians prescribe a daily vitamin-mineral supplement for children to be taken at mealtime. It is recommended that such supplements contain no added sugar, alcohol or artificial colorings.

TOOTH SAVER SUGGESTIONS TO PROTECT BABY'S TEETH

Dental problems start in infancy. Children with cavity-ridden baby teeth usually continue the pattern into adult life. There is enough knowledge today to create a cavity-free generation, but parents must take responsibility for their tot's teeth right from the start.

1. Parents should clean baby's teeth as soon as they start to come in. A piece of gauze will do the trick.
2. Don't fill the overnight bottle with either juice or milk—only water. Juice contains sugar and milk has fermentable bacteria.
3. Children should see a pediatric dentist before they are three years old—50 percent already have cavities by this time.
4. Children should be encouraged to rinse after every meal, floss once a day and brush as early as age three.
5. Sugary foods are tooth robbers.
6. Learning how to eat and swallow properly (without thrusting the tongue forward through the teeth) and avoiding lip and fingernail biting can prevent future need for braces.

ROLE OF HUSBAND

*"To become a father is not hard.
To be a father is however."*
William Busch
1832—1908

Judi was fortunate during her pregnancy to have a supportive husband in Jerry. This was especially true during the last two months when he had to take over the preparation of the food as well as help Judi with her daily exercises and household chores. Together they attended prenatal classes where they learned about correct breathing during labor, nursing and the importance of bonding for the father as well as the mother.

Jerry soon realized that the "average" baby would require 4,000 diaper changes in the first year which added up to 8,000 diaper changes for twins. Someone was going to have to help Judi with all those changes! (Jerry commented that he felt as though he had received a raise in salary when the twins got out of the diaper stage!)

Most fathers, if asked to fill out a "father application," would have to write in under *related training* or *prior experience* the word "unqualified," unless he grew up in a large household as the oldest son with "on the job training." But it's important to remember that, except for breast feeding, a father can be very capable in seeing to baby's needs.

For most couples, when the family changes to three—or more—shared parenting sometimes becomes difficult. Some mothers honestly expect to share parenting responsibilities equally with the husband, but when baby arrives, they cannot relinquish control even to a loving, caring husband. Mom should try not to engage in a power struggle, but learn to share responsibilities. Husbands should be willing to assume part of the physical caring of baby's needs and not assume that it's strictly a mother's responsibility. Work out compromises in caring for the new arrival when your feelings differ. It's a delicate balance, but a worthwhile goal.

A father who is actively involved in parenting makes for a better rested, more relaxed mother—which in turn makes for happier children. Children respond positively to a good relationship between their parents just as they are adversely affected by a bad one.

Increasingly, men are assuming more responsibility for their children and are finding that being with kids can be fun, exhilarating, creative and fulfilling—as well as exhausting, hectic, maddening, and frustrating. Sharing each of these feelings by being a fulltime partner with the mother provides unlimited benefits for those children who grow up in a two-parent family.

David Stewart, a father of five and a university professor, says being a success in fatherhood and career go hand in hand only if the father puts family happiness first. (Adapted from *Succeeding at Fatherhood* by David Stewart, *Family Journal*, Vol. 11, No. 3.)

Successful Fathering Tips

1. Respect your children as equals. Begin thinking in terms of this equality at baby's birth. Treat your children

with respect when they are young and they will treat you with respect when you are old. Adolescent generation gaps begin at birth.

2. Be at home as much as possible. Ninety percent of being a good father is being at home. Many problems can be solved with rapport which cannot be developed by parental absence. Absence has only one cure—presence.

3. Tune in to your family. Be at home in mind and spirit, NOT just in body. Never consider your time at home a burden or sacrifice nor spend it solely in front of the television. You cannot enjoy that upon which you have not placed your attention.

4. Love and touch your children. Learn to enjoy being with little ones. Everyone benefits. No father should be without a hammock—it's a perfect way to enjoy babies and little kids.

5. Don't pretend to know it all. If you want your words to be respected, they must always be respectable. Without credibility, there can be no communication. This means readily admitting, "I don't know."

6. Don't be afraid to show your shortcomings. Do not allow children to see one thing with their eyes and hear another from your mouth. Parents are the yardstick by which children measure the world.

7. Don't be overly concerned about consistency if change means a better way. Nobody is perfect. To remain constant throughout life is to make no progress. Be consistent in truthfulness, kindness and respect.

8. Don't insist upon an immaculate house. A home sprinkled with the objects of a child's play is a home scattered with the evidence of happiness. Childhood is a short time gift—enjoy children now. There will be plenty of time to enjoy a neat house when they're gone.

9. Don't pretend that father and mother agree on everything. Speak frankly and openly in mutual respect before your children, but remember that fighting or bickering in front of children is harmful.

10. Do unto your children what you would have them do unto others. Children are tape recorders of what they see, especially what they see in parents. Much to the embarrassment of parents, they often play back in public what they have recorded in private.

It is by example that we instruct children, not by words. Albert Schweitzer once said, "To teach by example is not the best. It is the only way." And the Bible commands *"Ye fathers, provoke not your children to wrath: but bring them up in the nurture and admonition of the Lord"* (Ephesians 6:4).

From the information in this chapter you, too, can be the Supermom and Superdad God intends by making your pregnancy what you want it to be—one filled with love for your baby. A child learns to read a parent's character before learning the alphabet. Parental and family ties form one of the most potent means God uses for converting others to Him. A godly home life is one of the best proofs of a true hope in Jesus Christ. Make your home the "heaven on earth" God intended for the nurturing of children.

4
Weaning Your Family from Junk Food

Did your reading, 'riting and 'rithmetic education leave a noticeable void in your eating know-how? This lopsided trio needs two additional R's—Righteousness (*"Man shall not live by bread alone, but by every word of God,"* Luke 4:4), and Rations (knowing what to eat is part of glorifying God with our bodies, I Corinthians 6:20).

Unhealthy eating habits do not develop overnight and improvements generally do not come quickly. Many families believe that making healthful food changes is a painful, punishing experience. Weaning families from junk foods can be done—not by decree, but gradually and with love.

Junk food addicts become so accustomed to the flavor and texture of processed, packaged and frozen foods that tastebuds have to be reeducated to enjoy fresh foods. Left to their own devices, some kids would exist quite happily on peanut butter—but only with grape jelly and always on white bread.

Every child seems to have at least one particular food hang-up or quirky food preference. Susie is on a monofood binge and eats only bananas. Mark trades his school lunch for sweet rolls and salty chips while refusing to eat the salad and raw veggies prepared by Mom. Jerry will eat anything that smells of burgers, fries and shakes. Mark devours colored cereals and bowls of corn chips while watching television. A different frozen dinner each night is Paula's idea of a perfect meal.

The older a child gets, the more questions are asked, and the greater the need for convincing, factual answers. What do you answer when asked:

"Why do we eat brown bread when my friends eat white bread?"

"Why don't we go to Burger King like Sheila's family?"

"Why don't we put salt on our food?"

This is the time when your nutrition education pays off. Kids are bright and they want answers. If they see foods sold via television by the Pepsi generation with slim, trim, beautiful, bouncing youngsters having fun, excitement and adventure, they are going to need knowledgeable answers for why they shouldn't consume the products. The average American child spends more hours in front of the television than in school and witnesses about 18,000 commercials for non-healthful foods.

One solution is to restrict the viewing of commercial television. (This can have more than one benefit.) Strengthen children's sales resistance when they watch commercial TV by pointing out gimmicks used by manufacturers to get people to buy products. Tuned-in kids are quick to unmask the sales pitch of the sponsor. Turn this into an educational, fun, family game.

What kind of health strategies can concerned parents adopt for teaching their children a sense of Christian stewardship for their own health? Creativity and a lot of psychology is required to unmask the sugar-coated messages beamed at children today.

The transition from junk food to healthy food can be painless when everyone is involved in a fun-filled adventure.

STRATEGY TIPS FOR CHANGE

Just "Forget"

Forget to bring home non-healthy foods. Remember out of sight is out of tummy.

Choose Good Snacks

Broaden the mind, not the body, by choosing snacks with chew power and high nutrient scores.

Push Vegetables

Gradually change to low-fat, high fiber meals and don't say, "Please try it. It's good for you." That's a sure killer. Just say calmly, "These are carrots. You might like them." Give kids a choice when possible. If you ask, "Would you like a spinach salad today?" an independent five-year-old may say "no." If you offer a choice between spinach salad and broccoli topped with chestnuts, you may get one vegetable eaten. Sneak spurned vegetables into soups, stews, pizza and spaghetti sauce. Grate carrots or zucchini and add to muffins or waffles. Serve *skinnywiches* with sprouts or dark leafy greens replacing lettuce.

If milk is the problem, try making frothy blender

shakes which include a favorite fruit. Slip non-fat dry milk (rich in calcium) into soups, custards, puddings or baked desserts.

Use a little psychology. Foods that help you "run faster" or "jump higher" sound and taste better than those "good for you" foods that look and taste yucky. Don't be surprised when kids pick apart tuna casserole, or can spot a potato buried under a mound of sauce or the celery in chicken salad. Some kids pick the raisins out of muffins and the sunflower seeds out of cookies—another reason for pulverizing these nutritional goodies before adding them to the batter.

Moms who do not like to say "no" will often give in to the demand for sweet, salty or fatty foods. Kids develop unholy power when they refuse to eat and an insecure mom pushes bigger and sweeter desserts or snacks.

By making an issue out of uneaten food, parents find themselves in a power struggle with family tyrants who discover that this is a great attention-getter. It's better not to make a fuss about the nutritional assets of peas or the hungry children of the world. Kids are not interested in such things. Parents should not take it personally or feel that they have failed if children refuse vegetables or milk. Encourage healthful eating by not giving in to childish displays of self-will. Anti-food strikes or monofood binges usually end after a few weeks.

Serve kids appealing, plain, raw or crunchy steamed vegetables. Or, give them an unmade sandwich with all the fixings and let them make their own lunch. At breakfast, set out eggs, pancake batter, cold cereals or fruit and tell everybody to be their own short-order cook. The night after a party, have a last-scraps buffet. Thin the left-over dip with yogurt for salad dressing. Slice the roast beef and set out mustard, bread, tomatoes and garnishes. Arrange bowls of "untossed" salad vegetables for a make-your-own salad.

Don't hover over food as if you expect kids to suddenly grab their throats and leave the table. Act natural. After a variety of food has been eaten, avoid a triumphant smirk. Nonchalance is the psychological key.

Play to Their Senses

Kids like colorful foods. Bright rows of orange carrots and green beans, broccoli "trees," or cookie-cutter sandwiches have kid appeal. Place a melon wedge on a plate of salad greens for a "Sailboat Salad." The name you give a dish can tweak the imagination and tickle the appetite. For example, apple "cookies" (the crispy, thin inside slice of an apple) and banana milk (a blender whip of banana, ice and low-fat milk) may be met with more enthusiasm than their plain counterparts. Keep in mind that looks count, too. Youngsters often seem to find cheese and meat more appealing when cubed or rolled up on toothpicks than when served flat on a plate. The same goes for yogurt and fruit when it's combined and frozen as "sherbet."

Think Small

Avoid big fights over little appetites. When growth spurts slow down, so does the appetite. During the first year when babies triple their weight and increase their length, the demand for nourishment seems endless. As the first birthday nears, appetite wanes as growth spurts level off.

Serve Mini-Portions

The one-year-old needs an average of 1000 calories a day which increases 100 to 200 calories a day each year until the age of seven. Too many kids are turned away from food by adult-sized portions. A balanced supply of nutrients—a half-slice of whole wheat bread, a few tablespoons of meat and vegetables or a half cup of milk is all little appetites can handle at one time.

Outsmart a Peanut Butter Rut
If your child has eaten only "peanut butter-and" sandwiches for weeks while refusing to touch vegetables or milk, search for nutrient-similar foods he will eat. There is nothing inherently superior about the vitamins and minerals in vegetables that cannot be found in fruits or the calcium in milk which is also in yogurt and cheese. You can even "doctor" the beloved peanut butter by stirring in calcium rich dry milk, sweet carrots, applesauce or a thin puree of fresh fruit. It's the nutrients kids need, not a specific food.

Ease Through the "Arsenic Hour" by Being Prepared
For moms and toddlers this usually occurs around 5:00 p.m. For school-aged kids, the arsenic hour occurs around 3:00 p.m. The hungry youngster reaches for whatever is handy. Smart moms use hunger as a positive motivator and keep only healthy alternatives on hand.

Let Hunger Build
Mealtime will be met with greater enthusiasm if you play to a hungry audience. In general, two to two-and-a-half hours should elapse between meals for young children. This works out to be three regular meals and two mini-snacks spread over a day.

Don't Push Sugar
Avoid using food for reward or punishment. Bribes

such as, "Finish this for mommy," or "No dessert till you finish every bite," often back-fire and produce an opposite effect like more cravings for the forbidden food.

Keep Mealtime Pleasant

The atmosphere at the family dinner table can have a profound effect on whether a child develops a positive or negative attitude toward eating. The evening meal is usually the only meal that many families share together and this should not be turned into a battleground or a time to unload all the day's problems. Keep tensions and stress away from the dining table. Encourage family interaction by banning television viewing or other distractions. Begin the meal by joining hands around the table and asking the blessing. At an early age have children fold their hands and thank God for their food.

Children who are made to feel ashamed or guilty at mealtimes may develop a negative attitude when Mom or Dad says, "Get your elbows off the table" or "Your report card was terrible—you don't get dessert." This creates an unappetizing atmosphere wherein children unconsciously associate unpleasant experiences with eating. Some children react to this kind of stress by turning away from food entirely or by turning to forbidden foods.

Keep mealtime a happy, relaxed, communicative time as well as a pleasant and satisfying experience.

Take Kids to the Supermarket

You can avoid being sabotaged here by adopting smart shopping techniques. Junk foods are always strategically placed to catch the eye of candy-loving children. Many well-intentioned parents are worn down by children screaming for cookies or candy from their perch in shopping carts. Make a shopping list before going to the supermarket and include children's suggestions when possible. They will be more willing to stick to the list if they have a say in making it. Tell kids that you won't buy foods not on the list. Decide ahead what treats will be purchased. When kids discover that wheedling and whining long enough will get them what they want, you usually lose every battle. Be firm and refuse to be bullied.

One clever mom practices what she calls the "front-end-load" approach before shopping with kids. She serves them nutritious "appeteasers" before leaving home to ward off the hungries.

Involve kids in label reading when they are old enough to read. Teach them that "first is most" in the listing of ingredients. Buy only those foods with "no sugar added." Look for labels that spell out the amount of sodium, saturated fat or cholesterol. Explain why you choose one brand over the other. Even a three-year-old will understand that you don't buy certain things because they don't help her grow up strong and healthy.

For example: "I want you to have healthy teeth. That's why I don't let you eat all the candy you want." My favorite twins have been impressed since the age of three that certain foods can give them a "fat tummy." This works like magic with them. (Developing a fat tummy is a health no-no with them even at this early age!)

Let children help select yogurt or produce. Teach them to smell a cantaloupe, count out cherries, rap a watermelon, bag up the grapes or hold the potatoes.

Back home from shopping, involve children in putting food away. This provides another opportunity for working and sharing. The job is finished faster with lots of hands so why not enjoy some vegetables and a special dip when you're finished?

Get Kids into the Kitchen

When delicious whole wheat bread was first served at school to elementary children, I was horrified and dismayed to see so much of it returned uneaten. The few exceptions seemed to be those children whose families ate whole wheat bread. About to panic trying to solve this problem, I was relieved when a first-grade teacher presented a plan that is a sure winner—get kids involved in simple cooking. They usually eat what they prepare even if the result is a "lumpy" failure.

Cooking provides children with a real sense of accomplishment. It also helps to release emotional responses. They love hands-on or hands-in experiences and cooking develops many skills. In addition to being fun with a lot of learning, there is a built-in benefit—eating. Let the little ones handle food as soon as possible—a few banana slices on the high chair tray or a dollop of banana peanut butter spread. Watch the intense absorption while tiny fingers touch and fondle food. Very little supervision from mom is required for getting food from the refrigerator, washing, drying or tearing salad vegetables, washing fruit, breaking beans, counting carrots, measuring dry ingredients, kneading dough or making play dough ornaments for the holidays. Even loading and unloading the dishwasher is a learning experience.

Moms and Dads fortified with courage and patience can encourage children to prepare the evening meal one night a week. Or what words could be sweeter than, "Mom, I made my own breakfast"?

RULES FOR WORKING IN THE KITCHEN

1. Always wash hands. Keep dish towels, pot holders and a tasting spoon handy.
2. Dress properly. Use an old shirt, apron or smock to cover clothes.
3. Read the recipe and get all the ingredients together.
4. Discuss the dangers of hot stoves, ovens, plugging in cords with wet hands; how to use a knife, stir in a pot, or how to remove lids from pots to avoid steam, and how to use a cutting board, graters or the blender.
5. Clean up food dropped on the floor so that no one slips. Never re-use it!
6. Use pot holders or oven mitts and turn all pot handles to the rear of the stove.
7. Help children remember that the stove stays hot even after the off button is pressed.
8. Keep a first-aid kit, broom and dustpan handy.
9. Put away all ingredients and clean as you go.
10. Enjoy eating together what you have prepared.

Along with grocery shopping, label reading, baking, and helping to prepare the meals, children are fascinated with growing and drying food. Children discover in growing their own salad vegetables or herbs that plants need many of the same things that people need—food, light, rest, warmth, water and plenty of loving care.

Ecological awareness becomes a positive learning experience as youngsters learn how to replace what they take from the earth when gardening. They enjoy using a food dehydrator for preserving foods for future use. A dehydrator is a valuable tool for getting kids into preparing healthy snacks as well as drying green grapes into raisins, banana slices, apple rings, fruit leathers, croutons, herbs and flower petals for pot-pourri. Eating dried food is the easiest and most pleasant part. Try it, you'll like it.

EATING OUT

Can a family make healthy choices when eating out? Yes. Ignorance is not bliss, however, when you eat out. Arm yourself with willpower, eating savvy and nutrient consciousness when eating out. Restaurant owners are finding that they have been forced to become more health conscious due to the fitness revolution spreading through the United States. Have you noticed the increase of salad, vegetable, potato, fruit, pasta, soup or taco bars at the fast food restaurants?

How can a person eat out without sabotaging healthy eating? Here are some suggestions.

1. Find ethnic, nouvelle or vegetarian restaurants. Many of these offer fresh foods, better cooking methods, more low-fat, low-salt and low-calorie choices. Some restaurants even have nutrition information available.

Oriental restaurants generally have a wide range of low-cal choices served with steamed vegetables and rice or noodles. Dishes that end or begin with "*nabe*" are fish or chicken cooked in broth. Low-fat specialties include hot and sour soup (minus meat), spicy chicken, steamed shrimp dumplings, vegetables, bean curd, fish, chow mein or scallops. Avoid sodium-laden soy-sauce or mono-sodium glutamate (MSG). Choose fresh fruit for dessert.

The Good Earth chain of restaurants offers Mexican,

Indian, Mid-eastern and Oriental menus with pre-
servative-free foods and baked goods made with
unrefined flour.

Italian restaurants offer a challenge in order to avoid
fatty cheeses, meats and sauces. When possible,
choose pasta with marinara sauce, lots of vegetables
and Parmesan cheese.

2. Fast food restaurant items generally lack fiber,
vitamins A and C, and are high in calories, fat, sugar and
salt. Go for those restaurants that have fish, salad or
vegetable bars, pasta, baked potatoes, soup or fresh
fruit. Skip the butter, mayonnaise, tartar sauce, catsup,
mustard or olives to save calories. Steer clear of
pickled, salted or canned foods as well as these fat
traps:

Bacon bits	1 ounce	188 calories
Cheddar cheese	1 ounce	100 calories
Macaroni salad	½ cup	170 calories
Potato salad	½ cup	150 calories
Croutons	1 ounce	110 calories
Corn relish	scoop	158 calories
Chick-peas	½ cup	360 calories
Bleu cheese	1 tablespoon	50-100 calories
Thousand Island dressing	1 tablespoon	50-100 calories

(Corn on the cob, served at several fast food outlets, contains
only 27 fat calories and 11 milligrams of sodium.)

Cheese pizza offers a better nutritional choice when
made on a whole wheat crust. Skip the pepperoni and
fatty meats. For purists, replace some of the cheese
with Parmesan. A typical slice of pizza has 15 percent
protein, 27 percent fat and 58 percent carbohydrates.

3. As soon as you sit down in a restaurant, order a
vegetable relish tray. The radishes and carrots keep
your hands busy and out of the bread basket. Better

still, have the bread basket removed unless it's whole grain bread.

4. Choose clear soups or broths. Avoid pates, cream soups or thick sauces which are heavy on the salt. Request that sauces, gravies or dressings be served on the side. Try squeezing on fresh lemon juice instead.

5. When ordering vegetables or potatoes, ask for baked or steamed—not fried. Stuff pita bread with fresh vegetables. Top with yogurt.

Potato toppers to choose include: grated cheese, chopped eggs, cottage cheese, tofu, yogurt, diced turkey, chicken cubes, vegetarian chili, sliced green onions, purple onion rings, toasted sunflower seeds, soy nuts, sesame seeds, peanut granules, fresh parsley, chives, basil, cucumber cubes, sliced radishes, shredded carrots, marinated peas, broccoli, cauliflower, diced green peppers, croutons, tomato cubes, crushed taco shells or sprouts.

6. Select lean meat, roasted chicken or turkey, or broiled, baked or poached fish, and ask the chef to hold the butter.

7. Pass up the non-dairy creamers. Ask for shakes made with fruit and low-fat milk.

8. When it comes to desserts, skip them or share with a friend. If fresh fruit is not on the menu, ask if it is available.

Don't worry about backsliding. It happens to everyone. With love and a smile, keep providing interesting foods that crowd out fake kinds of food.

Many families adopt the *Feeling Good Calendar* of positive health changes and keep it taped to the refrigerator as a healthy reminder. *Expect a miracle!* Keep the positive health changes happening.

FEELING GOOD CALENDAR

January
Develop an eating awareness plan. What triggers you to eat? Set realistic goals for your healthy image or the "new you." Assess, take action and go for it. Read a book on nutrition.

February
Go natural with whole fresh foods such as fruits, vegetables, seeds or chestnuts, Adopt a game plan when going to a party. Pre-load on a light snack. Do some exercises before going to a party to oxygenate the body. You'll eat less. Drink a glass of water before eating anything. Never go to a party hungry or tired.

March
Shake salt. Too much sodium causes the body to deplete potassium. Taste before adding salt. Be a wise consumer. Look for salt on labels. Stock up on herbs, curry or garlic powder, lemon or lime wedges, vegetable bouillon, onion flakes or toasted sesame seeds to use in place of salt.

April
Fuel up with fiber. Rough it with whole grain breads, unpeeled potatoes, oatmeal, bran muffins and dry beans.

May
Break for breakfast not doughnuts. Make breakfast your most important meal. Include protein for vitality and energy enough to avoid mid-morning fatigue.

June
Food for sport. What constitutes healthy food for sports and fitness? What should an athlete eat for a pre-game meal? Which beverages are best for replacing fluids? Practice Togethercise, and work as a family to answer these questions.

July
How dry I am. What do you drink when thirsty? Are you drowning your thirst in calories, caffeine, colas or chocolate? Sodaholics who drink one 12 ounce can a day add 55,000 *empty* calories in one year. Keep your cool with healthy thirst-quenchers.

August
Rate your child's school for fitness and nutrition. Does the school give a screening test for obesity, inflexibility or muscle coordination? Ask about their nutrition program. Plan now for snappy brown bag lunches.

September
Switch to healthy snacks. Keep raw vegetables, fruits, popcorn, toasted pita wedges, nuts, oat cookies, bean dips, sesame sticks, partially thawed frozen grapes or raisins, or raw fresh peas handy. Give plaque a whack with tooth-saver snacks. Make a list of 25 tempting snacks each with less than 100 calories.

October
Start a new fitness habit. Organize a healthy eating workshop. Keep a diary of food and exercise. Take brisk walks. Don't waste time in front of the TV. Strap on some ankle weights and lift those legs. Exercise is an emotional thermostat.

November

Be fat free. Choose low-fat cheese, cottage cheese, milk, yogurt, dry milk powder and low-cal salad dressings. Save 290 calories by switching to green beans instead of baked beans. Don't be a FAT/SUGARPUSHER. Replace the sugar bowl with sprinkle-ons of dried fruit, dried carrot curls, zucchini cubes, sweet potato rounds, date rocks, carob nuggets, sweet spices or grated orange.

December

Happy, healthy holidays. Planning ahead can make this season the happiest and healthiest of the year. Decide what is best for you and your family as opposed to doing everything your families have done in the past or copying the fairy tale productions in magazines or on television.

Low-stress activities provide time and energy for concentrating on the true meaning of the season—the birth of Christ through whom we have salvation and whose message brings love, peace and joy.

5
Nutritional Switching

What family does not have a spouse who is counting calories, children who have strong food likes and dislikes, busy work and church schedules, travel or family celebrations? With a little know-how, Mom can perform many nutritional tricks that will keep her family in the "pink of health."

Making family meals as nutritious as possible—with no one noticing—means sneaking in nutrition through some simple addition and subtraction. Now don't do what one eager mom did. She became so zealous that she overloaded all of her recipes with wheat germ which is a "no-no" in any family. Or another mom who cleaned her pantry of all junk food and gave it to her neighbor!

Families do not have to give up all their favorite foods in order to eat for better health. Unless there is a health crisis in the family which requires changing one's eating patterns as prescribed by a physician, most favorite recipes can be adjusted with healthier ingredients. Learn to combine nutrition with pleasure.

Modify recipes, alter cooking habits—and be a smart shopper at the supermarket.

There is nothing wrong in sneaking in nutritious foods your child won't otherwise eat or by boosting the nutritional value of the foods they do eat. Just don't tell 'em it's good for them!

DE-FAT THOSE RECIPES

Exercise mind over platter and switch from fat traps to heart savers with these tips:

1. De-fat omelets, quiches or other egg dishes by using 1 whole egg plus 2 egg whites. Egg whites contain no fat or cholesterol, only high quality protein.

2. Steam or wok-fry vegetables until crunchy tender. Use a stainless steel insert basket in a saucepan for stovetop steaming. Cook fast with high heat in stir-frying, sauteing or broiling. Keep the temperature to a low simmer when braising, stewing or roasting.

3. Think non-stick with low-/or no-oil cooking. Flash-stir vegetables in a non-stick skillet or wok with a tablespoon of sesame seeds (47 calories). The seeds release oil when heated, add flavor and calcium, and eliminate the need for additional seasoning. If you insist on using butter or oil, don't pour. Just fill a plant mister bottle with your favorite oil and lightly mist.

4. Fight fat and trim lean. Select lean meat, fish or poultry. Trim off all fat and do not add fat in cooking. Do not baste or brush with oil. Drain meat or towel blot it to remove fat.

5. Prepare meats, stew, sauces or soups ahead and refrigerate so that fat hardens and is easy to remove. Make no-fat gravy by using de-fatted broth thickened with oat flour. Make your own soups from scratch since canned soups are high in fat and sodium. Choose broth based soups minus the fat rather than cream based soups. Switch to gazpacho soup (1 cup) instead of the same amount of onion soup and save 130 calories.

6. Eating a meal with meat? Include fat-fighter vegetables such as carrots, onions or garlic. Include a dark green leafy salad loaded with vitamin C for better iron absorption.

7. Switch to low-fat dairy products. Is there milk intolerance in your family? Try kefir or acidophilus milk. Get acquainted with yogurt, the low-fat, calcium-booster. Even the Biblical patriarch Abraham served his guests curd or yogurt *"Then he took curds and milk and set before them"* (Genesis 18:8). A scoop of plain low-fat yogurt contains 16 calories compared to sour cream's 60 calories and whole cream's 200 calories. Create your own fat-free instant breakfast by blending fruit, skim milk, yogurt or protein powder. Top off this blender meal with whole grain crackers or muffins.

8. Look for labels that spell out the amount of saturated fats and cholesterol in the products. Saturated fat in the form of palm or coconut oils lurks in commercially baked breads and cakes, non-dairy creamers, french fries—even in granola.

9. Nuts to Nuts. Most nuts are heavy with fat, but they are a good source of protein. Choose chestnuts, soy nuts, almonds, walnuts, pistachios, pecans, or sun-flower. Eat moderately. Or fill your snack bowl with fresh peas.

10. Stretch peanut butter by stirring in grated carrots, applesauce or pineapple. Choose the old-fashioned peanut butter with no sugar or salt added.

11. Spread on nutseed meal for protein, calcium, niacin and fiber. Place raw almonds, hulled sunflower, pumpkin or sesame seeds in the blender and pulverize only until smooth. Mix nutseed meal with water and use on cereal. Refrigerate nutseed meal in airtight containers.

12. Watch butter and hard margarine consumption. Tub margarines are soft since they contain unsaturated liquid oil as the main ingredient (the first ingredient on the label). Butter Buds is a low-fat powdered butter substitute made from natural products. Sprinkle Butter Buds on vegetables or potatoes for a buttery taste minus the unwanted fat, cholesterol and calories.

13. For chocoholics who would "rather fight than switch," substitute 3 tablespoons of unsweetened cocoa plus 1 tablespoon of safflower oil for each ounce of baking chocolate. A healthy alternative for chocolate is carob. Carob pods grow on trees in the Middle East and also thrive in California. Tradition has it that John the Baptist ate this fruit in the wilderness. When the prodigal son ate husks that were for the swine, those husks were carob pods that had fallen from the locust trees (Luke 15:16). Carob contains two percent fat compared to chocolate's 52 percent fat. Carob has no caffeine and is rich in calcium, potassium, magnesium, silicon and iron. Be sure to buy only the "no sugar added" carob.

14. Skinny-down your recipes by going for whipped, popped, puffed or meringue air-fluffed foods. Pumping up volume means more for less. For instance, a regular dinner roll has 88 calories while a one ounce fluffy pop-over has 50 calories but looks like more. Foamy

souffles or mousses have fewer calories than pies or puddings. Eating angel food or sponge cakes saves 200 calories of fat over chocolate cakes's 312 calories. (Substitute oatmeal, raisins or carob chips for one-half the chocolate in chocolate chip cookies.)

15. Instead of two brownies, have two large oatmeal cookies and save 80 calories of fat.

16. Instead of a doughnut have a bran muffin and pocket 130+ calories.

17. Instead of broccoli in cheese sauce (1 cup), have steamed broccoli (1 cup) and save 85 calories. Go for thin sauces.

18. Instead of potato skins stuffed with extras (4 oz.), have a baked potato and save 310+ calories.

19. Set out a low-fat dip with raw veggies for an appetizer. Try carrots, peppers, celery, broccoli, cauliflower, string beans, cucumber, tomatoes and zucchini. Keep trimmed and washed vegetable munchies and fruits in the refrigerator for family "snack attacks."

20. Watch out for the salad bar. A salad bar meal is not a vaccine against fat and can stretch the tape measure to a whopping 2070 calories or shrink it to a firm 207 calories. It all depends on how you toss it:

● "Leaf" room for potassium-rich salad greens. Pile on a mixture of romaine, leaf lettuce, endive, bibb or fresh spinach, and go easy on the dressing. Substitute oil-free salad dressings instead of oil-based. De-fat dressings by using more vinegar or lemon juice and less oil. Stretch mayonnaise by using 1 part yogurt to 3 parts mayonnaise.

● Reeducate family tastebuds accustomed to vegetables covered with dressing by providing a choice of snow peas, red cabbage, fresh bean sprouts, marinated zucchini, asparagus, cauliflower, broccoli, tomatoes, green beans, celery or cucumbers. Everyone will be so busy crunching, they won't notice less dressing. Staying healthy was never so tasty since so many garden patch vegetables contain an extra bonus of both vitamins A and C.

● Build up a salad with healthy toppings such as pumpkin or sunflower seeds, cashews, almonds, walnuts, prunes, raisins, wheat germ, shallots, green or red peppers.

● Prepare salads just before serving. Also, delay cutting up and cooking vegetables until the last minute to reduce the loss of vitamin C.

21. Does your family go for cheese? In the Old Testament David is recorded as taking ten cheeses to his brothers in the army of Israel (I Samuel 17:18). Job refers to "curdled cheese" known today as cottage cheese (Job 10:10). Cheese lovers need to choose cheese wisely and compare their favorites for fat, sodium and calorie content. One fat-trimming trick is to mix a high fat cheese with a lower fat cheese. Try using less Cheddar cheese in a recipe and seek out semi-soft, low-fat (made from skim-milk) cheeses such as Monterey Jack, Muenster, Swiss, mozzarella, ricotta, farmer, string, Somerset, goat, hoop or dry cottage cheese.

Select uncreamed cottage cheese or rinse creamed cottage cheese lightly with water to remove fat and sodium. Substitute tofu for cream cheese. Tofu mixed with low-fat yogurt and non-fat dry milk makes a tasty spread but without the fat. Season with lemon juice or a favorite herb. Tofu can be grilled as patties or burgers and the fat-free tofu hot dog contains only 79 calories.

For the taste of cream cheese, try cutting the fat by blending ½ cup cream cheese with ½ cup of ½ percent low-fat cottage cheese.

GRAMS OF FAT PER SERVING OF CHEESE

Fats That Spread Around

4 ounces cream cheese	42.4
1 cup sour cream	48
4 ounces Cheddar	37.6
4 ounces Monterey Jack or Muenster	34
4 ounces mozzarella, part skim	24.5
4 ounces ricotta, whole milk	16
4 ounces 4 percent cottage cheese	4.7
4 ounces low-fat plain yogurt	2.1
4 ounces 1 percent fat cottage cheese	1.0

BOOST YOUR FLOUR

Making flour more nutritional is limited only by your imagination. Combine varied flours such as oatmeal, potato, whole wheat, rye, millet or cornmeal to add taste and increase nutrients.

Make your own nutritional flour. Add ¼ cup of wheat germ, soy flour and non-fat dry milk to ¾ cup unbleached white flour. Whole wheat flour can be interchanged with white flour, cup for cup, or go "halfsies" and use one-half of each until your family makes the grain transition.

Add a handful of dried fruits, granola, zucchini, grated onion, crunchy seeds or crushed herbs to muffins or pastries and increase protein, calcium and vitamins as well as offer a change of texture to baked goods.

How to Substitute For White Flour

1⅜ cups barley flour = 1 cup white flour
1 cup corn flour = 1 cup white flour
⅞ cup corn meal = 1 cup white flour
⅜ cup potato flour = 1 cup white flour
⅞ cup rice flour = 1 cup white flour
1 cup rye flour = 1 cup white flour
1 cup rye meal = 1 cup white flour
1½ cups ground rolled oats = 1 cup white flour
1 cup whole wheat flour = 1 cup white flour

Important! Always use a double portion of baking powder when converting a white flour recipe to dark flour. Average use is 2½ teaspoons baking powder to each cup of flour.

You can increase pizza protein by adding soy flour to the crust or by sprinkling soy flakes on top. The amount of protein in a pizza is increased by 30 percent simply by adding soy flour. Soy flour has more lysine, an essential amino acid, than wheat flour. The browner the pizza crust, the more lysine is destroyed.

Corn flour or arrowroot thickens sauces as well as cornstarch and it is healthier. It can be used in the same proportion as white flour. It also combines well with other flours in making muffins. Also, instead of using flour or cornstarch to thicken soups or stews, cook a few potatoes, place in blender until smooth and add to soup.

"SHAKE" SALT

Re-train your taste buds. Instead of shaking salt from your shaker, "shake" salt entirely and substitute your own blend of herbs and spices. Try Italian herb seasoning, five spice oriental powder, make your own from ground ginger, cinnamon, anise, nutmeg and cloves, or use one of these favorite blends.

I. 3 ounces dehydrated vegetables
   ¼ teaspoon garlic powder
   ⅛ teaspoon thyme
   ¼ teaspoon white & green onion powder
   ¼ teaspoon paprika
   ⅛ teaspoon ground celery seed
   ¼ teaspoon dry mustard
   ½ teaspoon pulverized parsley

   Place all ingredients in blender and blend thoroughly. Makes ½ cup.

II. 1 tablespoon cinnamon
   1 tablespoon curry powder
   1 tablespoon dried coriander
   1 tablespoon savory
   ½ teaspoon freshly ground parsley
   2 tablespoons powdered ginger

   Combine thoroughly and place in an airtight jar. Makes ⅓ cup.

Be creative as you cook and add variety to your saltless or less-salted dishes with any of the following flavor enhancers.
● Ground toasted sesame seeds or sesame oil.
● Unsalted, dry nuts and seeds such as caraway, poppy, or sesame add flavor and crunch.
● Grated lemon or orange peel. Quick-sprinkle over chicken, fish or squash.
● Frozen juice concentrates.
● Peanut or olive oil.

● Herb vinegars.

● Red bell peppers, horseradish, garlic onions, green onions, chives or leeks.

● Paprika and curry add zest, color and taste.

● Leaf herbs like basil, bay, dill, marjoram, mint or oregano give super flavor. Discard them before serving if you wish.

● Soy sauce is now available in a low-sodium version. Mix with equal parts of lemon juice for a basting sauce.

● Eliminate garlic salt, onion salt, seasoned salt, monosodium glutamate (MSG), Worcestershire sauce and bouillon cubes.

● Read labels for sodium content which can be found everywhere—even bottled water.

Where the Sodium Is

Apple 2 mg.*	Applesauce, 1 cup 6 mg.	Apple Pie, 1/8 frozen 208 mg.
Chicken, 1/2 breast 69 mg.	Chicken Pot Pie, frozen 907 mg.	Chicken Dinner, Fast-Food 2,243 mg.
Corn 1 mg.	Corn Flakes, 1 cup 256 mg.	Canned Corn, 1 cup 384 mg.
Cucumber, 7 slices 2 mg.		Dill Pickle 922 mg.
Lemon 2 mg.	Soy Sauce, 1 tbs. 1,029 mg.	Salt, 1 tsp. 1,938 mg.
Peas, fresh 1 mg.	Peas, frozen 115 mg.	Peas, canned 236 mg.
Pork, 3 oz. 59 mg.	Bacon, 4 slices 548 mg.	Ham, 3 ozs. 1,114 mg.
Potato 5 mg.	Potato Chips, 10 200 mg.	Instant Mashed Potatoes, 1 cup 485 mg.

Steak, 3 ozs. 55 mg.	Jumbo Burger, Fast Food 990 mg.	Meat Loaf Frozen Dinner 1,304 mg.
Tomato 14 mg.	Tomato Soup, 1 cup 932 mg.	Tomato Sauce, 1 cup 1,498 mg.
Tuna, 3 ozs. fresh 50 mg.	Canned Tuna, 3 ozs. 384 mg.	Tuna Pot Pie, Frozen 715 mg.
Tap Water, 8 oz. 12 mg.	Club Soda, 8 oz. 39 mg.	Sodium Bicarbonate in Water 564 mg.

* mg. = milligrams   Source: U.S. Department of Agriculture

"SUGAR-FREE"

You don't have to starve your sweet tooth—just re-train it. Most recipes call for more sugar than is actually needed and usually in combination with high calorie fats. Generally, sugar can be reduced by one-third to one-half and never be missed if you simply increase or add non-fat dry milk powder, flavorings of vanilla or cinnamon, or replace part of the liquid with fresh or frozen fruit juice. For sweetness minus the sugar, add a few drops of peppermint, vanilla, almond or orange extracts. Experiment to determine what is actually needed.

Don't be fooled by "sugar-free" or "reduced sugar" on labels. Sugar can still be a major ingredient, sometimes listed on the label in more than twelve forms.

Plenty of so-called "natural" products have a "no sugar added" label but have added citrus or orange concentrate which has sugar in it. Be sure to see which sugar-free form is used—aspartame, sorbitol or xylitol. All are chemicalized sweeteners and even though they cut calories, they do nothing to help you overcome sugar cravings. There have been no human or mammalian studies on aspartame to evaluate the mutagenic or carcinogenic effects of the methyl alcohol contained in it. If predictions are correct, it won't be long before an additional 2,000,000 pounds of it will be added to the food supply.

Painless Trade-offs for Sugar Cheats

1. Nature's ideal sweetener is fruit—fresh or frozen. Use fresh fruits, when possible, in dessert preparation. When buying frozen fruits choose the "dry" form without added sugar. Blenderize fresh or frozen fruits and use as a liquid substitute in most recipes.

2. Dried fruit is delicious when chopped, diced or sliced and added to baked goods, in fruit cups or skewered with fresh fruit for finicky appetites. Dates, raisins, prunes, apricots, figs, currants and pineapple can be pulverized in a blender or food processor and added to whole grain flour. Be sure when purchasing dried fruit that it has not been dipped in white sugar. Dried fruit can also be soaked overnight in water or skim milk which yields a rich, sweet-tasting liquid for use on cereals or in baking.

Soak dried apricots, golden or dark raisins, apples, dates or currants in fruit juice for 5 minutes. Add to cooked cereal in the last few minutes of cooking.

Remember that dried fruit is more concentrated than fresh—4 slices may be a whole apple.

3. When purchasing fruit juice concentrates, purchase it unsweetened and substitute it for the liquid or oil in baking cookies and breads.

4. Use coconut curls, slivered cashews or pulverized granola or cookies as toppings for various parfaits. Also mash fresh fruit and ricotta cheese for toppings.

5. Carrots, yams and acorn squash are unbelievably sweet and can be shredded, grated, mashed or juiced for adding to breads, cakes, cookies and pies.

Craving cake? Switch to fresh apple cake or carrot cake and reduce the sugar or honey by one-third. Joanna and Claire's birthday cakes are carrot or fresh apple cakes decorated with cream cheese frosting and pureed raspberries—delicious! Other cake alternatives include banana, pumpkin, date, zucchini bread, sponge cake or angel food cake.

6. Unsweetened applesauce or apple butter is a kid pleaser when mixed with peanut butter as a spread for waffles, muffins, cookies or crepes.

7. Replace jams or jellies with unsweetened fruit butters.

8. Make your own granola instead of using the store kind which may contain sugar, sodium and fat.

9. Switch to agar, unflavored or diet gelatin for jelled salads or desserts and replace part of the liquid with pure fruit juice. Avoid the highly sugared, artificially colored and chemically flavored gelatins.

10. Use diluted syrups on pancakes, crepes or waffles by thinning the syrup with water or fruit juice. Use sparingly a blend of blackstrap molasses, honey or pure maple syrup. Avoid maple-flavored syrups.

Molasses and sorghum contain more B vitamins, potassium, iron, calcium and magnesium than eight ounces of milk.

11. Honey is nature's oldest sweetener and in Biblical days was used as a substitute for gold when paying taxes. In fact, there are over 65 references in the Bible to honey and the honeycomb. In Luke 24:42

Jesus ate honey with His meal. *"And they gave Him a piece of a broiled fish, and of an honeycomb,"* and Proverbs 25:27 warns us against eating too much honey.

Honey is a whole food and when unfiltered or uncooked contains no chemicals. Due to the enzymes diatase, inulase, catalase and invertase, honey is digested slowly, does not irritate the lining of the stomach and has readily available energy. Honey contains calcium, magnesium, potassium, B vitamins, some vitamin C and a trace of protein. Honey is sweeter than white sugar so less is needed. Honey also contains more calories per tablespoon than sugar since it is more concentrated.

Sweetener	Calories per Tablespoon
White Sugar	46
Molasses	46
Honey	64

It is recommended that maple syrup, molasses, sorghum or honey be used sparingly.

How to Substitute for Sugar

Honey:

½ - ¾ cup honey for each cup of sugar	Reduce liquid in recipe ¼ cup for each cup of honey used.

Molasses:

½ - ¾ cup molasses for 1 cup of sugar	Reduce liquid in recipe by ¼ cup for each cup of

molasses used. Add ½ teaspoon baking soda and decrease the baking powder by 2 teaspoons.

Date sugar:
1 cup for each cup of sugar

Replaces dried fruits in cakes and cookies. In baking, add date sugar to the liquid and allow to stand for 10 minutes before combining with other ingredients.

12. Frozen desserts. Here is the "scoop" on ice cream and other frozen desserts.

Ice Cream. There is no substitute for that cool, smooth rich delight gliding down your throat on a hot summer day! But most commercial brands are too embarrassed to list their ingredients which may contain chemicals such as Diethyl Glucol (also used in anti-freeze). Even some containers contain chemicals to "preserve freshness!" Ice Milk has less fat than ice cream, but more synthetic ingredients plus more calories due to extra sweeteners added.

Fat-Wise	*Fat grams per cup*
Regular ice cream, 10% fat (½ cup = 27 milligrams cholesterol)	14.9
Soft Ice Cream	18.3
Ice milk, 5.1% fat	6.7
Sherbet (from scratch)	1.2

So what's an ice cream lover who wants a nutritious lick to do? The only way to insure control of ingredients (and lower fat) is to make your own—kids love taking turns cranking the churn. (Or suggest to Grandma a gift of one of the electric or new, quick freezing machines.) Try some of these nutritious, less sugared treats.

Banana portable cream. Peel bananas and cut in half. Insert a flat stick in each cut end. Dip in lemon water and roll in nuts, granola or sesame seed. Place on tray in freezer until frozen.

Portable shortcake. Ice cream cones are fun nibblers and edible cups. Fill cones with fresh fruit and top with real cream. (Encourage outside eating.)

Waffle cone sundaes. Fill a lacy waffle shaped into a cone with ice cream and topping of fresh fruit, nuts and seeds. Try toasting two homemade frozen waffles, scoop ice cream (or yogurt) on one waffle and top with second one. Eat quickly.

Fruit Pops. Most kids flip over finger-lickin' homemade fruit ice pops which are a frosty replacement for the nine teaspoons of sugar in an average serving of sherbet. Freeze fruit juice in popsicle cups or in an ice cube tray. Insert a popsicle stick when partially frozen or let thaw slightly and eat with a spoon.

Sherbets or ices. Use fresh strawberries, lemons, limes, pineapple, watermelon or papaya for light, fat-free ices. Generally these are blended and frozen for one to two hours until slushy, then removed from freezer and blended again until smooth and creamy. Refreeze until ready to serve. Serve in melon boats, orange cups or pineapple shells and garnish with small balls of fruit.

Sno cones. Blend 1 small can frozen fruit concentrate and ½ cup water. Add 8 to 10 ice cubes, one at a time and whirl until frosty. Pour into paper cups for a treat.

Quick-dip sherbet. Place a container of unsweetened pineapple chunks or peaches in the freezer. When frozen, mix in blender until icy smooth. Spoon into parfait glasses and garnish with fresh berries.

Fat-free sherbet can be made by blending 1 cup buttermilk, ½ teaspoon vanilla, ½ cup pureed strawberries and lemon juice to taste. Freeze in ice trays. Serve in a party glass with a fresh strawberry and sprig of mint.

Soft-serve yogurt. This is a lighter dessert, smooth and creamy. Choose yogurt made from skim milk. One cup of plain vanilla frozen yogurt has 180 calories. Fruit flavors are higher in calories.

6
Fat-Proofing Your Kids

Nine-year-old Tommy is a nice looking child. He is usually pleasant, tries hard to please and is generally liked by his peers even though he gets a lot of teasing and is called "fatty," "roly-poly," or "pudgy." He doesn't like these names and when he feels very sad, a candy bar usually makes him feel better.

Tommy doesn't enjoy being overweight and he really does not like himself very much. His parents and family say that it's baby fat and that he will outgrow it. Tommy believes his parents and knows that "one day" he will be thin. His present eating habits do not do much to encourage this image, however.

For example, he wakes up too late to eat breakfast, so he grabs some cookies and eats these while waiting for the school bus. During class he has a hard time staying awake and concentrating on the teacher's reading instructions. He sneaks a quick bite of candy stashed in his desk.

At lunch time he heads for the cafeteria where he

downs a hamburger, fried potato patties, cookies and chocolate milk. During physical education class he plays volleyball with his classmates but can't move as fast as they can, so he chooses to sit on the sidelines most of the time.

Following school he returns home to watch television and eat the cookies Mom has waiting for him. During dinner he doesn't feel too hungry but eats the meatloaf and macaroni casserole. He cleans his plate in time to see his favorite television program. Before going to bed he has some nachos, dip and a glass of milk.

Does this sound familiar? If your child's eating habits are anything like Tommy's, then it's time for some changes. You can't wait for a chubby child to outgrow fat. Fat cells acquired in childhood usually last a lifetime. There is evidence that childhood obesity is a significant risk factor for adult obesity. Childhood fat endangers one's physical and mental well-being and social growth as well as future educational development and career opportunities.

Obese children suffer damage to their self-esteem and show undesirable personality characteristics such as passivity and withdrawal. Even loving parents play a part in the fat child's low self-image. Few parents paste pictures of a fat child in the family album or on the refrigerator door. An overweight child is teased, rejected, and sometimes the object of ridicule or hostility at school.

Dr. Gerald Berenson of the Louisiana State University Medical Center states that there is clear and extensive evidence that heart disease begins in childhood. Research over the last 30 years shows that the progressive buildup of plaque on arteries begins early in life.

The National Children and Youth Fitness Study funded by the U.S. Department of Health and Human Services in October 1984, found that today's kids are fatter than those of 20 years ago and that they don't get enough vigorous, prolonged physical activity to maintain a strong heart and lungs. Other findings of the study included: (1) Enrollment in physical education classes declines as students get older (98% in fifth grade; 50% in 12th).

(2) Only 36.3% of the students take P.E. classes daily.

(3) Only 47% of class time is spent on activities that can readily be carried into adulthood.

(4) Exercise patterns are seasonal, with fall and winter activity roughly half that of spring and summer.

Researchers concluded that a concerted effort by schools, community organizations, children, and parents is needed to meet 1990 federal goals and to improve the health and fitness of American children. The President's Council on Physical Fitness states that most adults in America are in better shape than this country's youth.

The American Health Foundation, a non-profit research group, found that 25 to 30 percent of school age children have dangerously high cholesterol levels— above 180 milligrams. Ideally a child's cholesterol level should be 110 milligrams though up to 140 milligrams is considered safe. The current average for children? A high 160 milligrams.

The National Institutes of Health Consensus Development Conference Statement on *Health Implications of Obesity* cites the implications of obesity as an "enormous psychological burden" connected to a variety of illnesses such as hypertension, diabetes, coronary heart disease, certain cancers and longevity.

The report panel viewed with concern the increasing frequency of obesity in children and adolescents and stressed the urgency to increase the understanding of obesity in order to start a program of prevention in early childhood.

CAUSES OF OBESITY IN CHILDREN

Fat is neither fit nor healthy. What causes children to be fat and unhealthy?

1. Overfeeding an infant. During infancy Mom confuses giving the "best" with the "most"—the most attention, devoted care and all the food baby wants. Breast-fed babies are seldom overweight while bottle-fed babies often are. (The doctor "ordered" the whole bottle to be fed to baby.)

2. Starting solid foods too early—before four or five months of age. Many pediatricians advise caution and gradual introduction of solid food, one food at a time, to prevent later allergies.

3. Pressure by Mom for baby to eat more teaches baby that food pleases Mom or Dad.

4. Keeping a toddler confined to a playpen or stroller which curbs movement and exploration activity.

5. Encouraging a child to watch television or to have quiet tea parties (with sweet treats) instead of jumping rope or bicycling. Sometimes fat families own three television sets, two cars, one fat pet and no bicycles or roller skates.

6. Giving in to a child who whines for sweets in order to gain a few minutes of quiet.

7. Using food for comfort, consolation, reward or punishment. Food cues are emotional and are associated with special treats, reward snacks or of special foods when one is sick.

8. Keeping a refrigerator stuffed with tempting leftovers within easy reach of a toddler or cabinets loaded with foods containing no nutrients, only calories. Having bowls of candy or high-fat munchies in the living room. Storing ice cream in the freezer by the gallon.

What can you as a concerned parent do to help your children avoid obesity?

HOW TO AVOID CHILDHOOD OBESITY

The Christian mother realizes that she is the guardian of her family's health. It is usually Mom who decides what foods to buy at the supermarket; Mom who does most of the meal planning and food preparation, and Mom who has the most control over the child's food intake.

Many parents are in better shape than their children. As you exercise at the gym, you remind yourself that you are growing fitter each day, but what about the kids? Are they in shape? Nagging or telling a chubby child not to eat is counterproductive. So is saying "go play" unless parents set the example.

To help get your children on the road to fitness and health, adopt these four positive P's—planning, participation, perseverance and prayer. And avoid the four negative P's of push, pressure, punish and pester.

PLANNING

Check with your family doctor to determine what your child's weight should be and whether or not a weight loss plan is needed. Weight gain is usually gradual, caused by overeating a little day by day. Most children can adjust to the idea of *not* gaining anymore weight rather than being attacked for gaining too much. Their self-image is very fragile and the idea of being put on a diet is regarded as some sort of punishment.

Develop with the child a behavior modification plan. This means helping your child unlearn habits that caused fatness and learn new eating and exercise habits that lead to slimness.

Keep a simple food diary to determine exactly what is eaten, when it is eaten and what triggers the urge to eat. Let children who are old enough to write keep the diary.

Keep the food diary for several weeks as a means of tracking calories. Once a week discuss with the child the successes or failures of what the diary reveals. Give praise for successes, however small. Be casual and make no comment when goals are not reached. Stress your child's abilities—never the shortcomings.

Constant encouragement such as "You're doing great" or "I know you'll get it next time" will keep spirit and interest high. Avoid setting yourself up as a police figure.

Keep the lines of communication open and periodically ask yourself "Who am I doing this for?" If the answer comes up "Me," you need to reconsider your motives.

Give some kind of reward for changing habits but don't offer food or money as the reward. Instead, offer special privileges such as staying up one hour later on weekends or spending more time with you, the parent, in a special project or activity.

Decide together what realistic goals are to be set for the following week—maybe switching to fresh fruit for a bedtime snack. The Feeling Good Calendar in chapter 4 provides some excellent ideas for getting started.

Be sure you leave a column in the food diary for day by day activity—the games played, chores completed, how many times the stairs were used over the elevator or the number of miles walked, jogged or cycled.

PARTICIPATION

Make fat-free eating a family affair. You know the facts about fat and heart disease. Is your husband as trim and healthy as he was when you married him? Maybe fewer/fat-free calories could help him, too. How about you?

Family support is extremely important to an over-weight child and provides needed reassurance. If Mom or Dad is overweight, too, the child learns to balance caloric intake with caloric expenditure right alongside Mom or Dad. Children who slim down with their parents are more successful at losing pounds and keeping fat off permanently. Children cannot be expected to control their weight when there are bad examples all around them.

Plan family meals that are nutritious for all members of the family. Adjust individual portions based upon activity, age, size and other factors so that the chubby child does not feel deprived or punished.

Remove all food-related chores from the child such as preparing food or clearing the table.

Establish a routine of sit-down meals with relaxed family conversation and *no* television or book reading while eating.

Short-circuit the cookie connection by keeping healthier substitutions available at kid height. *You* eat them, too.

Trim Calories and Be Pound Wise. Here are several ideas as starters:

1. Check out seeds, nuts and dried fruits. One ounce of raisins equals 166 calories compared to a 1.8 ounce candy bar with 233 calories.

2. Choose pretzels (unsalted) as a snack. One ounce yields 100 calories while potato chips have 120 calories per ounce. Dry roasted nuts have about 160 calories per ounce while oil roasted ones weigh in at 170 calories per ounce.

3. Avoid thick, smooth foods like gravy, sauces, cream cheese or sugary desserts.

4. Choose watery, crisp and bulky foods like tomatoes, radishes, celery, cucumbers, melons or salad greens.

5. Keep a grab bag stuffed with raw veggies handy. Tuck in a surprise.

6. Serve fresh fruit kabobs.

7. Switch to low-calorie salad dressings or make your own using tomato, vegetable juice, or lemon juice instead of oil.

8. To an 8-ounce container of plain yogurt, stir in fresh fruit, unsweetened cereal, low calorie jam, vanilla extract or unsweetened applesauce. For a change of taste, stir in ¼ teaspoon of vanilla extract to flavor plain yogurt or low-fat cottage cheese. Remember that frozen yogurt has about six percent more sugar than ice cream.

9. Enjoy Fruit Frappe. Place ¾ cup fresh straw-berries, ¾ cup pineapple (fresh or unsweetened, canned) and several ice cubes in a blender. Blend until smooth. Pour into a parfait glass and garnish with a fresh strawberry. Yummy!

10. Evaporated skim milk whipped as a topping saves 646 calories per cup over regular whipped cream.

11. Popcorn is a favorite high fiber, sugar-free munchie. One cup of unbuttered popcorn contains 50 calories. Taste teasers to add to popcorn include:

Parmesan cheese
Grated orange or
  lemon rind
Melted unsweetened
  carob

Dried apple rings or
  banana chips
Shredded wheat bits
Cheerios
Toasted wheat kernels
Unsalted pretzels

12. Nutritious nibbles with less than 100 calories:
● Yogurt—½ cup plain low-fat yogurt with straw-berries and peaches = 80 calories.
● Cakes and Butter—2 rice cakes and 1 teaspoon peanut butter = 98 calories.
● Curly Sandwich—1 lettuce leaf, a slice of thin ham, a scallion = 49 calories.
● Vanilla Wafers—5 cookies = 75 calories.
● Frosted Grapes—Freeze 1 cup of grapes = 45 calories.
● Almond Joy—16 almonds = 60 calories.
● Super Shake—⅔ cup buttermilk blended with ½ cup blueberries = 90 calories.
● Swiss 'N' Rye—2 Rye Krisps with slivers of Swiss cheese = 90 calories.

- Cucumber Boat—scoop out center of cucumber half, fill with low-fat cottage cheese, and top with pimento slices = 62 calories.
- Chilled Dip and Veggies—½ cup plain low-fat yogurt spiked with chili powder or dill weed plus assorted fresh vegetable slices = 100 calories.
- Baked Apple—core a medium sized apple, stuff with raisins and a sprinkling of cinnamon and bake = 83 calories.
- Cold 'Choke—one cooked and refrigerated artichoke with 1½ tablespoons of low-calorie mayonnaise = 75 calories.
- Cider—6 oz. hot apple cider with a cinnamon stick = 62 calories.
- Fiber up—1 cup 40% bran flakes cereal = 106 calories.

13. When kids ask to buy high calorie foods, show them how to use a calorie counter and have them look up the number of calories in the food.

14. Use a score card and "star" the foods that have multiple nutrients and lots of chew power.

15. Tape a colorful calorie food chart at eye level on the refrigerator.

16. Remember that it takes 30 minutes for the stomach to signal the brain that it's "full."

PERSEVERANCE

By this time most of the snacking and mealtime problems should be under control. There will be problem spots which require patience and perseverance to solve. But work on these areas as promptly as possible. Generally it requires 21 days to establish a new habit. Even if it takes more time than you expect, remember that habits changed over a long period of time are more likely to stay changed.

Children and fitness are natural partners. The activities are endless—so are the rewards.

1. Continue to help improve your child's self-image. Make a list of ten things that you like about him or her—and keep the list handy. Forget about past failures and concentrate on the new understanding of one's body and what caused the excess weight in the first place. Refuse to become frustrated. Stand firm as you create a positive environment for learning and changing.

2. Keep a boredom grab bag handy. Fill it with assorted colorfully wrapped toys, mini-books or puzzles. Allow your child to select one when boredom strikes.

3. Help the child to acquire new social skills. Following the rules, working on a team with others, perseverance and self-discipline encourage a positive self-image.

4. Give love and encouragement freely.

An unhappy child becomes a potential fitness drop-out. Parents know their children best and need to encourage and provide positive experiences along with generous amounts of loving support to help children grow up fat-free.

PRAYER

Through prayer and meditation, ask God to show you what is desirable and pleasing to Him. *"Perseverance must finish its work so that you may be mature and complete, not lacking anything. If any of you lacks wisdom, he should ask God, who gives generously to all without finding fault, and it will be given to him"* (James 1:4-5). Ask God to guide you toward the foods that are best for your family.

As you change the foods that you serve to your family, what about the foods you serve to your guests? If that fattening dessert is unhealthy for your family, should you serve it to friends?

Discipline is necessary in order to be the kind of follower God wants us to be. This includes becoming the master of all our appetites—particularly of food. Just as the abuse of alcohol, sex or drugs is a sin, so, too, does God's Word condemn gluttony, the abuse of food.

God wants us to master our appetites and to be filled with the Spirit. If we ask God for control, God will answer. *"And this is the confidence that we have in him, that, if we ask anything according to his will, he heareth us"* (I John 5:14).

STEP UP PHYSICAL ACTIVITIES

Many weight problems do not necessarily come just from overeating but also from a lack of physical activity. Americans have tried to improve upon the laws of God as applied to physical movement by becoming dependent upon energy-saving conveniences. Do you realize that Jesus walked 50 miles from Gennesaret to Tyre and Sidon (Matthew 15:21)? The people of Israel walked six miles on the march around the city of Jericho (Joshua 6:3-4), and Moses, at the age of 120, climbed Pisgah Peak on Mount Nebo (Deuteronomy

34:1). These activities of the men of the Bible give testimony to their robust physical stamina. We should accept no less in our physical conditioning.

1. Encourage movement at a very early stage in a little one's life—from creeping and crawling to jumping, tumbling and climbing for the two-year-old.

2. Make exercising together a fun, family hobby. Seek out those fitness classes that are available for toddlers and moms. Seeing my twin granddaughters Joanna and Claire "work out" with their mom is a hilarious and most rewarding experience. Their bends, twists, kicks, and stretches provide play exercise for them as well as valuable lessons in balance and equilibrium. Judi uses the twins as ankle "weights" when she does her sit-up exercises and they love it. "Togethercise" is healthy parenting both mom and dad can share.

3. Create a positive environment for exercise. Once a week go for a family walk or nature excursion. Encourage gardening and household chores. If team sports are spurned, try swimming, roller skating, badminton, tumbling, jogging, cycling, catch or softball.

4. Let your child decide what activities to pursue and respect their personal preferences. Keep instructions to a minimum. The goal is to give encouragement, not strive for perfection.

5. Try not to pass on your own physical fears or insecurities to your children. If you are petrified of the water, try to encourage their swimming lessons from a qualified instructor while you watch from the sidelines.

6. Include vacations in your behavior modification program. Vacations are a great time for family get-togethers but present a difficult time for counting calories. Encourage your child not to view the vacation

as an excuse for overeating but rather as the start of a fitness program. Make certain there are plenty of exercise activities available such as hiking, tennis, swimming, horseback riding or bicycling.

7. Check out the physical education program at your child's school. Is there at least one period of vigorous activity each day? Are there classes to develop sports that will last a lifetime like tennis, swimming, aerobics, golf, skiing, cycling or jogging? If your child's school does not have these, get together with other parents to form a plan of action. Enlist those church and community resources that are available.

8. Make weight training a family affair and keep a graph of each family member's progress. Make it fun to grow up fat-free. What you start today can have life-long benefits.

7
Teacher Says It's Okay

"Train up a child in the way he should go; and when he is old, he will not depart from it" (Proverbs 22:6).

Having been a classroom teacher before becoming the director of school nutrition programs, I have had many opportunities in these 31 years to observe and study the teacher-child interaction of "hands on" nutrition education. My experiences have been blessed by knowing many teachers who are Super Stars because of their love and devotion to children. There are some teachers who should have every second grade child in the country assigned to their classes!

It is generally acknowledged that during the critical early years parents have the most influence on their child's eating habits. Habits instilled during those years are not easily forgotten, peer pressure and television commercials notwithstanding, even when kids reach high school. Yet when children get to school "what teacher says" becomes very important and may supercede their parents' opinions.

COOPERATION IN TRAINING

Whether or not parents and teachers take an active role in shaping kids' eating habits depends largely upon how important they think eating really is to health. Until both the home and the school begin to apply the nutrition knowledge that is available, the children that they love will not be helped.

Because of my work in school nutrition, classes for parents, and in some cases in response to my *Nutritioning Parents Newsletter*, I receive many letters from concerned parents, teachers and students asking what they can do to provide this help in their situations. The following letters are typical.

How delighted I am to find a publication devoted to training parents toward healthy eating—and what clever ideas for summertime refreshment! How do I raise my two-month-old baby near my sister's child who receives her ton-a-day of sugar and junk foods in the typical American manner?

HELP! HELP! HELP! Please send information that I can include in a nutrition packet for my child's kindergarten teacher who serves a snack of cookies with a choice of chocolate or white milk (some choice). *I need cold, hard facts to educate this teacher who knows nothing about nutrition.*

One of my dreams is to have my children enjoy a healthy lunch at school. Congo bars are not my idea of a reward for eating a school lunch. I see neither progress nor change in the program and it saddens me.

My son recently entered first grade. The following is an example of his school lunch:

Cheeseburger on Bun (white bun)
French Fries
Lettuce, Tomato and Pickle
Brownie
Milk
Please send instructions on how to implement a nutritious lunch program in a public school.

(From a school superintendent:) I am working hard at improving our school lunches. I would greatly appreciate your sharing any materials and/or details and processes involved in establishing your innovative and successful program.

(From a second grade teacher:) I am writing because I would like several samples of your newsletter "Nutritioning Parents." As a primary school teacher I have close contact with parents and I feel many would be interested in your newsletter. I am also researching information on ways to improve our lunch program.

(From a high school student:) About a year ago I read an article in a magazine about enlightened school lunch programs throughout the country. Ever since, I have been interested in achieving something similar at the school I attend.

I am a diet conscious high school sophomore distressed at what I see students around me feeding their bodies each day. I would very much like to see the situation change. However, our school lunch program is not helping very much. Just recently the cafeteria removed the salad bar and replaced it with a hamburger relish line. Also, numerous kinds of empty calorie snacks such as potato chips, cinnamon rolls, candy bars, and pop, are available continually throughout the day at the student store.

I am co-vice president of my sophomore class and have helped organize a pro-nutrition committee consisting of other concerned students. We would like to see things change so that those of us who want a healthy diet may have it conveniently available. It is also our hope that through us others might become more educated in this field and be inspired to switch to more nutritional diets for their own well being.

It would be appreciated if you could send some information on how to go about this. Our committee is aware it may not be easy and we might meet with some conflicting attitudes but hopefully it will all be worth it in the end. Thank you!

I am a 3rd grade teacher and a "Naturalist Nut" trying to convert my kids and their parents. I need more "ammunition." Please send information.

I am a parent in a small town in Alaska. As you can see from the enclosed weekly menu printed in our local paper, junk food is served. I don't want my kids to have to eat hot dogs, white bread, etc., nor do I want my only option to be sending lunches and having my kids be the "oddballs" in a small town. Please help.

I am very health minded. Now that I am confined to a wheelchair, it's so easy to gain weight. I have a son, Christopher, who had his first birthday one week before my accident. Now he has "three moms"—myself and both my parents. Mom (58 years old) finds it hard to break habits. Meanwhile Christopher is "hyper." Please send information so my parents will listen.

In this country we are very much behind the times in nutrition education. The authorities are only just beginning to wake up now that our appalling health statistics prove that we are the "sick man of Europe." Please send information on your Nutrition program.

And so goes the mail—endless, awesome, challenging, sometimes heart-breaking, but never dull. So many end their letters with "God bless you" which renews and refreshes my spirit.

How do parents and teachers turn "can't" into "can" for getting healthy changes made at school?

Are parents and teachers interested enough to examine the eating patterns of their kids? (Some parents are not aware of how terrible their kids' eating habits are.)

How can teachers begin kick-the-habit changes in their own eating patterns so they become good models of what is taught in the classroom?

How can children be motivated to track their own eating habits and assume responsibility for their own health?

The answer is a planned effort on the part of parents, teachers and students toward establishing better nutrition in their schools.

ALL-OUT INVOLVEMENT

Get everyone involved in the action and develop a strong network of support. Involvement by all concerned tells the child that they care and establishes a communication bond in a triangle approach between the home, classroom and cafeteria. Lack of understanding or cooperation between the triangle forces results in frustration and anxiety.

The Parents' Part

Parents benefit the most when they are needed and

share their talents with others. In 1983 the American Association of School Administration stressed "Three V's" that parents should do to get more involved in their child's education:

1. *Visable.* Attend parent conferences to get to know teachers. Join and support the school's parent organization. When children see that their parents think school is important, they do, too!

2. *Volunteer.* Provide extra touches to make the difference between good and great education. Children do better in school when parents are involved. Find out what jobs need to be done.

3. *Vote.* Be active and informed. Vote in school board elections, attend board meetings and finance meetings.

There are three additional "V's" for parents to adopt for the sake of better learning and better nutrition:

1. *Visit.* Have breakfast and/or lunch with your child at school on more than one occasion. Ask about the school's nutrition program. Check out what the teachers eat for lunch. Are any soft drink, candy or ice cream vending machines in the building? How many teachers have jars of candy on their desks? Has a *Nutrition Letter to Parents* been sent home requesting that parents not send gooey candy, cookies, cakes, chips, soft drinks or pre-sweetened colored drinks for school parties? See the sample *Nutrition Letter to Parents* which follows.

SAMPLE NUTRITION LETTER TO PARENTS

Dear Parent:

During this school year your child will be involved in an exciting FEELING GOOD PROGRAM and COME ALIVE NUTRITION at school. Every effort is being made to instill in all students basic nutrition knowledge needed to help them make wise food choices now and throughout life.

Learning what to eat and why is an essential part of a child's education.

COME ALIVE NUTRITION PROJECTS are being planned for classroom and cafeteria activities.

You may be receiving some "take home" materials to encourage your involvement in our nutrition program. It will be important for students to practice at home those concepts learned at school.

In accordance with the Southern Association for School Accreditation, the National P.T.A., the International Reading Association and the American Dental Association, only those foods and beverages that contribute to health are to be consumed at school. Therefore we seek your assistance and cooperation in providing healthy foods and beverages containing no artificial colorings or caffeine, and those which are low in sugar, fat and salt for school breaks, meals or classroom parties.

You can understand why it is important that foods and beverages for parties, snacks and meals contribute to the good health of your child.

We have included some suggestions for nutritious party and snack food.

If you have questions or would like more information, please let us know.

Sincerely,

2. *Volunteer.* Offer to serve as a "Snack Mommy" to promote healthier snacks and school parties, or as a nutrition aide to assist teachers. Sponsor a "Nutrition Workshop for Moms and Dads" to provide training for classroom cooking, storeroom tours, label reading, sugarless snacks, health surveys, fitness fairs, floating nutrition libraries, dental health, and ethnic meals at school. Get the parents' cooperation in preparing a *Teacher's Nutrition Action Packet* and present it to teachers at the beginning of school.

SUGGESTIONS
For Contents of the Teacher's Nutrition Action Packet

(A) A monthly calendar of nutrition projects or changes. Be sure to list available resources such as health oriented speakers, films, etc.

(B) A list of fund raisers for school projects to use as alternatives for candy and doughnuts.

- Light Bulbs
- Mugs
- Singing Telegrams
- T Shirts
- Gift Wrapping Paper
- Marathons
- Car Washes
- Huggable Stuffed Toys
- Fashion Shows
- School Telephone Directory Sales
- Pencils
- Spiral Notebooks
- Duffle Bags
- Stickers
- Wallets
- Flowers, cut or potted
- Singing Carols
- Fruit
- Greeting Cards
- Job Coupons
- Hair Cuts
- Pizza Nights
- Concerts
- Picnics and Barbecues
- Computer Dating Service
- Book Covers
- Gym Shorts
- Shoe Laces

- Art Auction
- Nutritious Snacks
- Mistletoe Sale
- Tube Socks
- Cookbooks

The fund raiser alternatives are from my friend, Anne Condas and her special interest group, Better Educational and Nutritional Standards (BEANS) of the California Reading Association. Anne Condas, 17766 Hillside Court, Castro Valley, California 94546.

(C) A nutrition book list to encourage health awareness. A "floating nutrition" library enables parents and teachers to share reading materials.

(D) Free Field Trips. Check out the following in your area for an important stimulus in promoting nutrition education. (Be sure to include addresses, telephone numbers and the name of the person to contact for the free field trips.)

- Farmers' Market
- Food Processing Plants
- Grist Mill
- Food Salvage Banks
- Bakeries (A whole grain bakery in Atlanta has each child make their own mini-loaf of bread as a gift from their visit.)
- Gardens & Horticulture Center
- Fast Food Restaurants
- Orchards
- Natural Food Stores
- Ethnic Markets
- Farms and Fields
- Dairies
- Supermarkets

(E) Nutrition Letter to Parents. (See sample letter.)

(F) Mini-Nutrition Blurbs. These are short sayings that can be read by kids over the school's intercom system. Sample:

- Are You a Hot Fudge Sundae? You Are What You Eat. Is your behavior pattern like a hot fudge sundae— "smooth and creamy and sometimes bittersweet"?

Sugary Snacks create mood swings and put you in an energy slump.

● For a figure you can be proud of, stay away from the cheat list (sugary foods, potato chips, soda, pies, cakes.) Instead, substitute raw vegetables, fresh fruit, fish, chicken, plain popcorn, yogurt, kefir and low-fat cheese.

● Six cups of broccoli a day may take care of your calcium requirement. But who wants to eat six cups of broccoli a day? Try, instead, an 8-ounce plain yogurt with fresh fruit, a cup of milk, ½ cup broccoli, an orange, or a slice of whole grain bread. These are *action packed foods*.

● Did you know that one cigarette burns up 25 milligrams of vitamin C? All smokers need extra citrus fruits, fresh strawberries, cabbage, green peppers, tomatoes and dark green vegetables—even the peeling on your baked potato. Better yet, stop smoking.

● When jogging, doing push-ups, swimming, playing tennis or other sports, be sure to drink extra water or fruit juices to replace what is lost in perspiration. Also chew some pumpkin seeds to help replace zinc.

(G) Donate the *Kitchen on Wheels* to encourage classroom cooking projects. The *Kitchen on Wheels* is composed of two portable carts which go to classrooms. They contain mixing bowls, measuring spoons, a blender, portable mixer, cookie cutters, electric oven, crock-pot, peanut butter machine—even a food dehydrator. Equipment is donated, borrowed or purchased by parents and can be as simple or as elaborate as time and money permit.

Teachers are more inclined to do simple classroom cooking when utensils are accessible. Be sure to include nutrition charts, aprons and recipe books for preparing healthy snacks, breads, soups and sandwiches. (The sprout sandwich is a winner for pleasing kids—teachers, too.)

Arouse interest by having each class contribute nutritious recipes and put the best recipe from each class in a "Nutritious Nibbles" booklet. Of course each class gets to sample their winning recipe.

The Sprout Sandwich (sometimes called "The Disappearing Sandwich") is made by spreading two slices of whole wheat, cracked wheat or rye bread with safflower mayonnaise or yogurt. Place on the bread a thick layer of alfalfa sprouts. Top with thick pickle slices, finely shredded carrots, skinny cucumber slices and natural cheese. (A layer of sliced mushrooms can also be added.) Cut into finger sandwiches. Enjoy and watch the sandwiches disappear. (Kids like to grow the sprouts, grate the cheese, slice the cucumbers—even make the bread.)

(H) Gardening Projects. Gardening in school courtyards, under shrubbery or beside play areas provides valuable opportunities for growing your own vegetables, salad greens, and herbs as well as enjoying the harvest. Dry the herbs and sell to parents. Ecological awareness becomes a positive experience as kids learn how to replace in the earth what they take from the earth.

3. *Voice.* Be vocal and concerned. Encourage your children's schools to at least meet the National Dietary Guidelines for healthier meals for children.

Support the American Heart Association, the International Reading Association, the American Dental Association and the National Parent-Teacher Association (see Sources for information and addresses).

Promote the goal that only those foods that contribute to health be served at school meals, parties, snacks or concession stands and as fund-raisers. Encourage healthy refreshments at parent meetings also.

Be vocal with elected officials for support and commitment to make fitness and health curriculums that teach children how to take care of their bodies required courses. Urge the restriction in all school programs of those foods high in sugar, salt, fat and cholesterol. (Purchasing expenditures in some school districts reveal that students are receiving as much as 12 teaspoons of sugar a day at lunch time.)

Provide and share information through a newsletter for parents relating to nutritional information and suggestions for snacks and meals at home. (See the sample newsletter.)

When speaking up for your kids, be pleasant, positive and persistent.

The Teacher's Part

Teachers exert a tremendous influence on children—including the teacher's eating habits. Food education is not a "one time thing." An occasional lesson unit on nutrition will not provide the necessary incentive to students to improve their nutritional status, especially if the teacher's lifestyle does not back up the teaching. A reading teacher described the influence of teachers as "more caught than taught"—or to put it another way, "Thou therefore which teachest another, teachest thou not thyself?"

What nutritional and positive lifestyle habits are being taught in the classroom—intentionally or unintentionally? And what negative messages are coming across? Negative nutrition messages may be conveyed by the classroom environment, while the teacher is actually trying to communicate good health habits in class.

For example:

1. In the classroom the teacher stresses eating a variety of foods every day, yet walks into the cafeteria or hallway sipping a soft drink at lunch time.

2. When vegetables and fruits are stressed and sugar condemned in a lesson on health, these messages are contradicted by classroom cooking experiences of making candy and ice cream or the cafeteria selections include chocolate milk and marshmallow cake.

3. The importance of holidays is emphasized by parties with edibles of sugar-laden candy, cookies and cakes.

4. Teacher keeps a jar on the desk filled with candy or cookies to use for "special treats."

5. The bulletin board is decorated with the cookie monster eating cookies.

Be aware of the kind of nutrition materials used and what message is conveyed. (Industry "freebies" are no longer limited to skimpy pamphlets and cheap posters.) Health promotion projects should focus on teenagers' dieting and eating disorders as well as their exercise habits—with the teacher as a role model.

Teachers need nutrition information in order to change their own eating habits and those of their students. Usually, nutrition education is not a required course for becoming a certified teacher. Concerned parents can help to change the situation, if they approach the teacher in a friendly, sharing and intelligent way. Teachers placed on the defensive are not eager to help.

Some of the barriers parents may face when talking with teachers about nutrition are:

● A refusal to accept the responsibility for setting the health example for students.
● A reluctance to participate in self-improvement courses unless they receive release time, overtime pay or certification credit.
● An unwillingness to rewrite "old" lesson plans.

Most of these objections are understandable, but parents with a prepared solution to the problem can go a long way toward removing formidable barriers. Someone has said that, "Knowledge is like a rock set upon a shelf. It does no harm nor good so long as it rests there, but let somebody jar the shelf, the rock falls off and something happens." In 1978 I taught my first "Teachers Nutrition Workshop" in order to "make something happen."

The objectives of the 55 hour course (in cooperation with staff development for certification credit) were to provide basic nutrition knowledge for teachers, to create nutritional awareness, and to strengthen the linkage between home and school.

Dr. Lendon Smith's book, *Improving Your Child's Behavior Chemistry*, which we used as a textbook, helped teachers realize that the successful functioning of any individual depends upon the full nourishment of the brain. Dr. Smith was on hand to present certificates to the first teacher graduates of the course.

Some teachers confessed to me that meeting Dr. Smith was an incentive for taking the course the next time it was offered. Others credited the healthy snacks served before class as their incentive! (See

Sources for information about obtaining Dr. Smith's book.)

Parents who are serious about making a nutritional difference in their school can follow the same or similar plan.

The course includes:

1. A personal "make-over" of the teacher, which means looking at one's lifestyle and/or keeping a food diary. Some teachers may need to begin exercising, reduce caffeine intake, stop smoking, switch from the afternoon candy bar to fresh fruit, or plan a total behavior modification for losing weight.

2. Sponsor a nutrition project that involves students, parents and the school cafeteria.

3. Have "mini" nutrition times in the classroom on a daily and/or weekly basis. Teacher projects include:

- Nutrition and Behavior
- Creative Snacking
- Food For Fitness
- Breakfast Surveys
- Animal Experiments
- Nutrition Is Fun
- Weight Control for Teens
- Gardening with Mother Nature
- Bread Making
- Sprouting
- Labels May Be Hazardous to Your Health
- Foreign Food Day
- Sports Nutrition
- Protein Snacks and Learning Ability

The protein snack varies. Sometimes it can be a peanut butter ball mixed with dry milk, applesauce or orange juice, and rolled in sesame seeds; or stuffed eggs, cheese toast, fruit and a cashew dip. Many students and teachers skip breakfast and are more susceptible to infections, tire easily, have tendencies to depression and other emotional disturbances. Kids love making the morning protein snack and teachers enjoy the benefits.

The Students' Part

Students are communicators and for learning to take place they must be involved in the planning and evaluation. Students provide valuable input and spell success or failure for many school health and fitness programs. An effective students organization and action group is called SNAG—Student Nutrition Action Group, or SNAC—Student Nutrition Action Committee.

These groups can be sponsored by parents, teachers, principals, coaches, cafeteria personnel, ministers or health professionals.

Student projects for these groups include menu planning, food and purchasing surveys, health fairs, gardening, animal experiments (their findings are shared with other schools), consumer trips, kitchen tours to view food preparation which includes sampling and taste-testing new foods, snacking, family eating surveys, advertising and food choices, body image and obesity, health problems such as stress and hunger, decorative bulletin boards relating to health, and educational table tents placed on cafeteria tables. Popular tent topics for teens are:

- Want to lose weight? Don't skip breakfast.
- Avoid stress for good health.
- Keep fit to feel better.
- Food and skin.
- Food—the source of energy.
- The food you eat—on or off balance?
- To smoke or stop?
- Low-fat—Reduced Calories
- Fluids for replacing competition dehydration.

- Calcium for Bones
- Fiber for Fuel

Yes, you can turn "CAN'T" into "CAN" and enjoy the benefits of good nutrition in your school. Remember the grain of mustard seed (Mark 4:31-32)? I have witnessed many miracles in food education that began with one tiny seed. So can you.

8
Tooth Fairy Snacks

What is as American as apple pie but has never been seen in the nearly one hundred years of its existence? The *Tooth Fairy!* Yes, there really is a TOOTH FAIRY. In 1977, to my surprise, I received the *Tooth Fairy Award* for reducing the amount of refined sugar in meals served to school kids. The award was presented in— you guessed it—a tiny *Tooth Fairy* pillow edged in lace.

Tooth Fairy Snacks are snacks made up of complex carbohydrates and protein. Carbohydrates supply quick energy (which is one reason for snacking) and protein for prolonging the release of energy and providing satisfaction.

Snacking for health means saving about 20 percent of our daily calories for nutritious nibbles. Too many snacks come from coffee breaks, the "pause that refreshes," candy, salty chips or pretzels, none of which packs a nutritional punch. These kinds of snacks contribute to tooth decay, overweight, disturbed blood sugar levels, caffeine jitters and high blood pressure.

EVERYONE LIKES TO SNACK

● 40 percent of school aged children snack.
● Pre-teens and teens depend on snacks for up to 25 percent of their calories.
● Some 60 percent of all adults admit to consuming over 35 percent of their total calories in snack foods.

Snacking can make an important contribution in meeting energy levels provided they are well planned. Too many young adults rush around in a "starve and stuff" routine, though, then grab a snack to maintain energy. Most pre-teens and teens report they snack after school due to hunger, boredom, emptiness and activities that *require* food such as homework or television. Some admit that snacking fills the gap of loneliness when coming home to an empty house.

Many times older teens claim they don't have time to sit down and eat due to afterschool sports, clubs, job or home responsibilities. So they snack throughout the day. Their favorite snack foods include:

Candy	Chocolate	Ice Cream
Sodas	Pizza	Cookies
Doughnuts	Pastries	Peanut Butter,
Chips	Hamburgers	Jelly & Crackers
Fruit	Fries	

On the other hand, *Tooth Fairy Snacks* are good for you. The number of times you eat a day is not as important as what you eat. And making the transition to healthy tooth savers is not as difficult as it may seem.

The safest technique in making the transition is to keep only healthy snacks in the house. Of course, this may not solve the problem when your child asks, "Why don't we ever have good things like at Kevin's house? His mother always has candy for us—not apples." Unfortunately, kids learn very quickly to expect candy or bubble gum at the shoe store, drive-in window at the bank, gas station, Grandma's house—even when making a visit to the doctor's or dentist's office.

What happens outside the home is difficult to control but when something is brought into the home which you do not consider healthy, allow one taste or one selection, and put the rest "away." My daughter Judi, does this successfully with the twins.

But you can encourage health-conscious snacking, dodge the drill, and have healthier teeth, gums and smiles—with these *Tooth Fairy Snacks*:

1. TINY TOTS—offer finger foods such as teething biscuits, toast, ripe fruit (bananas, apples, pears, melons), cheerios (Place a few of these on the highchair tray and enjoy watching the child's maneuvers to reach the mouth!), unsalted crackers, bite-size shredded wheat.

2. TWO-YEAR-OLDS—enjoy celery stuffed with peanut butter mixed with applesauce and yogurt, pudding pops, crackers and cheese, juices, dry cereal in a cup, frozen bananas, bread sticks and spreads, mini-sandwiches, hard cooked eggs, cheese toast, raw vegetable slices, cottage cheese melt, banana bread with ricotta cheese and fruit popsicles.

3. PRESCHOOLERS—enjoy yogurt shakes, cheese, walking apple salad, nut mix, granola, fresh fruit, vegetable sticks, oatmeal cookies, "go with" sandwiches, whole wheat rollups, nutty nibblers, bran

muffins, yogurt popsicles, sno cones, popcorn, yum balls, dried fruit, cubes of meat, vegetable soup, crackers with nut butter, and pocket pizzas.

4. SCHOOL AGE KIDS—generally head for the kitchen when getting home from school, looking for "something to eat." Here are some *Tooth Fairy* ideas for them.

● Keep pancakes or waffles in the freezer. They can be toasted and served with applesauce and/or peanut butter.

● Have some broth in the refrigerator. Heat and spice it up with last night's leftover rice or noodles.

● Make mini grilled-cheese sandwiches. Just put a slice of cheese on a cracker and heat in the oven until the cheese melts.

● Serve up kid-size pizza. Lightly toast an English muffin, spread with tomato sauce, sprinkle with grated cheese and place in the broiler or toaster oven until the cheese melts.

● That old standby popcorn can be a new treat when sprinkled with grated Parmesan cheese.

● For a different warm-up drink, heat apple cider or apple juice. Don't forget the cinnamon stick.

● Skewered foods of all kinds are pleasers—melon chunks, pineapple wedges, cheese cubes, strawberries, meat cubes, cherry tomatoes or marinated vegetables.

● Pocket pizza is always a favorite. Fill pita pockets with mozzarella cheese. Top with mixed fresh vegetables. Bake at 350 degrees for 5-10 minutes.

● Apple Bread Pudding. Melt 2 tablespoons of butter in a skillet. Cube 4 slices of whole wheat bread and stir into the melted butter. Add 1 cup diced tart apple, ½ cup raisins and ½ teaspoon each of cinnamon and ginger. Mix gently. Stir together 1¼ cups milk and 2 tablespoons honey. Drizzle over skillet mixture. Cover and cook slowly until apple is tender. Spoon into 2 serving dishes. Top with yogurt.

● Hot Cranberry Toddy, serves 1. In a small saucepan heat 6 ounces of low calorie cranberry juice almost to boiling. Pour the hot juice in a favorite mug and add a wedge of fresh orange. For less than 40 calories you can drink all of it and have seconds.

● Nutty Bowl. Combine sunflower seeds, sesame seeds, dry-roasted unsalted peanuts, raisins, dried pineapple bits and carob chips in a bowl.

● Mexican Bean Dip. Cook about 3 cups kidney or pinto beans. Saute ¼ cup chopped onions, peppers (optional), parsley, and hot chili peppers; put all together in blender with lemon juice, cayenne, a little oregano and basil and mix until barely blended. Good with whole grain bread or vegetables. Low fat, low price, high nutrition.

● Cheesy Herb Popcorn. While popcorn is hot, grate in any of your favorite cheeses and herbs such as romano or curry.

● Easy Granola Bars. Mix together 1 cup natural crunchy peanut butter, 2 beaten eggs and 4 tablespoons honey in pan over low heat. When slightly warmed, add 2½ cups raw oats and 1½ cups mixture of sunflower seeds, raisins, carob chips. Oats are important, but the rest can be anything you like. Pat into 8 × 8 non-stick pan. Store in the refrigerator until ready to serve.

● Fruit and Peanutty Yogurt Dip. Slice apples, pears, and oranges. Serve with a dip of 8 ounces plain yogurt mixed with ¼ cup natural peanut butter. This dip is also good on salads, as a sandwich spread or with cut-up vegetables.

• Orange Julius. Place in blender 1 cup orange juice, 1 egg, ¼ teaspoon vanilla, ½ cup milk and ⅛ teaspoon nutmeg. Whip approximately 1 minute. If you whip it with ice, you will have a slush! Makes 2 servings.

• Banana Orange Frosted. Put in blender 1 cup orange juice, 1 cup milk, 2 bananas (cut up), and mix on high speed. Add 6 ice cubes, one at a time, until crushed. Makes 3 one-cup servings.

5. TEENS—snack primarily on what is available to them—whether at home, a friend's house or at their favorite fast-food restaurant. Parents can make certain that plenty of bone-building snacks are kept in the house, especially those that are easy to pick up and ready to eat.

Teens want to look and feel good, so food appeal can be based on looks, weight control or athletic performance. Take a trip to any school cafeteria and check out the number of teens trying to lose weight and the kinds of diets they have chosen. You can be sure somebody is either just starting a new diet, planning to start one on Monday, or admits they can't lose weight no matter how hard they have tried. Suzy, a tall blonde sophomore says she is on the "apple diet" as she crunches away on her third apple. Nearby, another student is on the "Vitamin Life" mixture which she pours from a thermos while admitting "it's gross." Across the way Irene is buried in a book, studying during her lunch hour while she continues her "food fast" or program of eating dinner only.

Teen years are called the "age of susceptibility" and these young people are eager to try almost anything—especially fad diets. Girls lead the weight struggle more than boys and often risk serious nutritional deficiencies for the sake of being thin.

There is no easy, fast or magical way to lose weight. What is taken in as food calories has to be balanced with activity output. We all must learn to "work off" those pounds before they build up.

Did you know that the 105 calories in a soft drink require 20 minutes of brisk walking, or 16 minutes of bicycling to work off; a candy bar (1½ ounces) at 220 calories requires 42 minutes of brisk walking or 38 minutes of bicycling to work off and a Big Mac (6½ oz.) at 545 calories requires 104 minutes of brisk walking or 84 minutes of bicycling to shake those calories?

Teens who are aware of their bodies will put the bite on "snack attacks" that just add up to fat and empty calories. Snacks for teens need to contain bone-building calcium, protein, iron, fiber, potassium and a smorgasboard of all the vitamins.

MORE HEALTHY SNACKS

What are some healthy munchies that are grabable, fast, guilt-free, energy boosters and good for healthy teeth, gums, smiles and dodging the drill?

● *FIBER*—your quick-fix toothbrush. Go for vegetables such as celery, cucumbers, zucchini sticks, cauliflower, leeks (split and trimmed), turnip rounds, broccoli, chinese snow peas, lettuce (romaine, iceberg, curly endive, escarole and red-leaf), spinach, watercress, green and red peppers, cherry tomatoes and cabbage. Also, add whole wheat bread, breadsticks, crackers, toast (but no jam), tacos, tortillas, corn chips and popcorn.

Be prepared with containers of freshly cut-up veggies in the refrigerator for nibbling. Counting calories? Eat plain.

Stuff pita bread with ready to go salad greens, radishes, mushrooms, peppers, water chestnuts, tomatoes and sliced green onions. Top with cubed or shredded cheese. Go for a glamour muffin—choose banana, bran, date, pumpkin or apple.

High fiber foods promote a strong cleanser action-flow in the mouth.

● *MILK.* Drink milk and cut back on soft drinks. Bone rich products like milk, yogurt and cheese are essential teeth-builders. Many teens may be short on calcium due to the consumption of too many soft drinks which contain phosphoric acid and deplete calcium. (See Chapter 2 for facts about cola drinks.)

● *CHEESE.* Try a cheesy sugar-chaser. Animal studies show that cheese may be tooth-protective when eaten along with sugar-charged foods. Cheddar and other aged cheeses appear to have even more of the ingredients that seem to protect enamel. Eat a cube of cheese as a snack chaser to a sugary food, or, European-style, after a meal to safeguard teeth.

● *FRUIT.* Feed your sweet tooth with various fruits. The total health benefits of fruit outweigh any risk to your teeth even though fruit contains "fruit sugar." Fresh fruits do not linger in the mouth like sticky, sugary foods. Switch to fruit parfaits, ambrosia, fresh melons, cantaloupe, grapes, pineapple, blueberries, raspberries, blackberries, strawberries, apples, oranges, grapefruit, pears, kiwi, papaya, mangoes and apricots.

● *FRUIT JUICES*. Processed fruit juices lack all of the nutrients of fresh fruits, including fiber, but they are still good foods. Juice drinks must contain 30 percent fruit juice. Avoid fruit drinks or ades which may be mostly colored sugar water. Flavored drinks can contain less than 10 percent fruit juice.

Artificially flavored drinks contain no fruit juice. Lemon and lime punches contain only six percent fruit juice. Ades must contain 15 percent fruit juice, except lemonade and limeade, which need only contain 12.3 percent juice.

Adapted from *Food Sleuth Handbook* by Sandra K. Friday and Heidi S. Hurwitz, Atheneum Publishers, New York, 1982.

Feed your gums. If you're not eating enough vitamin-C rich foods (citrus fruits, berries, tomatoes and broccoli), your gums could be in trouble. A balanced diet, including adequate amounts of vitamin C, helps your gums withstand bacteria attacks and protects against plaque buildup and periodontal disease.

What about sugarless snacks? Aren't they "cavity-savers"? There is some evidence that sorbitol sweeteners fuel mouth bacteria. It appears that sorbitol doesn't attack tooth enamel as rapidly as sugar, but eventually does cause decay. So overuse of sugarless gum or mints should be avoided.

SOME NUTRITIOUS SNACK RECIPES

Pocket Pizzas

Split whole wheat pita bread and top with 2 tablespoons of tomato paste, sliced vegetables, strips of cheese and sprinkle on parmesan cheese. Place in the toaster until the cheese melts. Enjoy.

Stack the Deck Pancakes

Ingredients: about 2 small, whole fresh yellow squash, cooked; 2 cups prepared dry pancake mix, ½ cup milk, 2 eggs.

Steam squash until very soft. Put all ingredients in a bowl except the milk. Mix with rotary beater, adding milk gradually until desired consistency is achieved. (This may require using more or less milk than recipe indicates.) Top with applesauce, yogurt, cottage cheese or crushed pineapple (unsweetened). Yield: 12-14 pancakes.

Note: Other yellow sweet squashes, such as butternut, can be substituted. This batter can be made the night before (after the kids are in bed) and stored overnight in the refrigerator.

Cottage Cheese Melt

To serve 1: 1 English muffin (whole wheat), 6 tablespoons low-fat cottage cheese, caraway seeds.

Preheat broiler or oven at 400°, split muffin and lightly toast. Spread cottage cheese evenly on muffin halves. Sprinkle with caraway seeds. Broil until cheese melts.

Morning Nog

To serve 4: 1 cup plain yogurt, 1 cup ripe bananas, peaches or strawberries, 1 tablespoon apricot or orange concentrate.

Mash fruit and combine with yogurt. Pour into freezer container. Stir until creamy. Serve frozen.

Sno Cones

Blend 1 small can frozen fruit juice concentrate and ½ cup water. Add 8 to 10 ice cubes one at a time while blender is on high. Blend until slushy. Pour into decorated paper cup. Serves 4.

Judi's Puffin

You will need 2 cups pumpkin; 2 eggs, beaten; 1 cup skim milk; 1 teaspoon cinnamon; ¼ teaspoon ground cloves; ¼ teaspoon ginger; ¼ teaspoon nutmeg; ¼ cup shredded coconut, unsweetened; raisins; red grapes or cherries.

Mix pumpkin and spices. Add eggs and milk until smooth. Spoon into 4 non-stick dessert baking dishes. Bake for 25 to 30 minutes at 325°. Combine coconut with 2 drops of yellow food coloring and 1 drop of cherry juice and a drop of water in a small jar with a tight lid. Shake until coconut is evenly tinted. Spoon 1 tablespoon of coconut partway around edge in each dish to resemble "hair." Add raisins for eyes and nose; cut cherries or grapes into sliver for mouth. Makes 4 servings.

Pepper and Onion Pizza

For a quick mini pizza, use 6 whole wheat English muffins, 1 8-ounce can tomato sauce, 1½ cups coarsely grated Cheddar cheese, ⅓ cup diced green pepper, ¼ cup diced onion.

Split muffin halves and toast cut-side-up under

broiler. Spoon tomato sauce evenly over muffin halves. Sprinkle with ¾ cup cheese, pepper and onion. Top with remaining cheese. Broil pizzas 6 to 8 inches from heat about 2 minutes or until cheese is melted and bubbly. Serve warm. Makes 6 servings.

Teacher's Favorite
Sneak in some extra nutrients and fiber to peanut butter with fruit. Use 4 slices of whole wheat bread or pocket bread, 6 tablespoons peanut butter, ¼ cup raisins or chopped pitted dates, 1 large apple.

Toast bread, if desired. Spread one side of 4 bread slices with peanut butter. Sprinkle raisins over 2 bread slices; press in lightly with back of spoon. Add a layer of apple slices; top with remaining bread. Cut sandwiches in half. Makes 2 sandwiches.

Glamour Muffin
You will need 2 cups unprocessed bran, 1 cup rolled oats, ¼ cup whole wheat flour, 2 teaspoons cinnamon, 1 teaspoon nutmeg, ¼ cup sunflower seeds, 2 eggs, 1 cup buttermilk, ¼ cup blackstrap molasses, 2 large apples, quartered (seeded but not peeled).

Preheat oven to 400°. In a large bowl, combine dry ingredients. Mix eggs, buttermilk and molasses in a blender. Add apples and blend until coarsely chopped.
Fold mixture into dry ingredients. Spoon batter into paper lined muffin tins. Bake 20-25 minutes. Makes 24. Wrapped, they stay moist in refrigerator for a week, or they can be frozen.

Portable Shortcake

Ice cream cones are fun for nibbling and are also edible cups. Using a cone for a cup, you can bake your favorite bran muffins, carrot or apple cakes and top with your favorite frosting.

Fill a whole wheat cone with layers of fresh strawberries and whipped cream. Top with a tiny strawberry and enjoy a yummy portable shortcake.

Nutty Crunch

Stuff celery sticks with ricotta cheese and sprinkle with crushed peanuts, sunflower or sesame seeds.

Apricot Candy

Use blender to mix ⅓ cup grated, unsweetened coconut; ¾ cup chopped nuts (almonds, pecans or walnuts); 1 teaspoon each lemon juice, grated lemon rind and orange juice; ¾ cup dried apricots, steamed 5 minutes in ½ cup water and drained; ½ cup wheat germ.

Shape into balls and roll in wheat germ.

Snack Kabobs

For each serving: 1 date, 2 cubes cheddar cheese, 2 walnut halves.

Spear a date with a toothpick, slide to the center of the toothpick. On either side of the date, put a cube of cheese, then a walnut half on each end.

Banana Freeze

Peel 2 small, ripe bananas, wrap in plastic wrap and freeze until firm. Cut into chunks. In blender container or food processor bowl combine banana chunks, ½ cup evaporated milk and ½ teaspoon vanilla. Cover and blend until smooth. With blender or food processor slowly running, add 1 cup frozen whole, unsweetened strawberries, a few at a time. Blend until smooth. Serve at once. Serves 4.

Breakfast Parfait

To serve 1, take ½ cup plain, low-fat yogurt; 1 teaspoon cinnamon; 1 cup strawberries, diced (reserve one whole berry); 1 ounce ready-to-eat cereal.

Combine yogurt and cinnamon. Alternate layers of berries, cereal and yogurt mixture in a parfait glass. Garnish with the reserved berry. (You may substitute different seasonal fruits and alter cereal choices for variety.) Serves 1.

Super Sundae

Blend 1 cup plain, low-fat yogurt; ½ banana, sliced; ¼ cup mixed nuts, unsalted; cinnamon or nutmeg to taste. Chill. Serves 2.

Strawberry Dip

Take 1 cup fresh strawberries, 1 container (8 ounces) plain low-fat yogurt, dash ground nutmeg, assorted fresh fruits.

Wash and hull strawberries. Place in container of electric processor or blender. Add yogurt and nutmeg.

Cover and blend until smooth.

Pour into serving dish. Serve with whole strawberries, cluster of seedless grapes and apple slices sprinkled with lemon juice to prevent browning. Makes 2 cups.

Portable Eggs

To serve 6, use 2 hard boiled eggs, shelled; 2 tablespoons mayonnaise and yogurt (mix half and half); 2 teaspoons mustard with horseradish; red pepper or pimiento.

Cut each egg into 6 wedges with a sharp knife. Carefully remove yolks from whites. Press yokes through a sieve into a small bowl; reserve wedges of whites.

With a fork, blend yogurt-mayonnaise, and mustard with horseradish into egg yolks to make a smooth paste. Spoon into white wedges and garnish with red pepper or pimiento. Refrigerate until nibbling time.

MIDNIGHT SNACKS

You wake in the middle of the night and your mind whispers "midnight snack." You toss back the covers and steal quietly to the kitchen, your ears pricked to every creaking floorboard. If you live alone, there's less sport to snacking, but if you have a mate or a roommate and must depend on the eerie glow of an open refrigerator for light, you should choose "quiet" goodies. Here are tips for keeping midnight snacking private—and healthy.

CLAMOROUS SNACKS TO AVOID

● Carrots and celery—they have a chomp that could wake the dead.
● Apples—a cacophonous crunch.
● Cereal—a roaring avalanche as it rolls down the box and crashes into a bowl.
● Bread—the crinkle of cellophane wrappers makes too much racket.
● Peanut butter—getting it off the teeth results in loud lip-smacking.

BEST QUIET TIME SNACKS

● Yogurt—eaten from the carton.
● Bananas—piece de resistance of soundless snacks.
● Applesauce—no crunch at all.
● Turkey—gnaw on a leg.
● Tortilla—spread on butter, hot sauce; roll it up for a soundless chew.
● Skim or buttermilk.
● Pre-made popcorn dusted with Parmesan.
● Fat slices of fresh zucchini topped with hoop cheese.
● Swiss 'n Cakes—rice cakes or wheat circles with slivers of Swiss cheese.
● Frosted grapes or raisins—as long as the freezer doesn't make a foghorn hum when the door is open.

9
Healthy Party Pleasers

Hooray for birthdays! A young child looks on birthdays as special occasions and bubbles over with anticipation as *his* day draws near. Even most adults enjoy the extra attention that a birthday brings. Being fussed over and having friends and loved ones show you they care is always nice. And how about the priceless look on someone's face when he walks through the door and everyone yells "Surprise!"

Birthdays create a "happiness occasion" for young and old that stores up memories for years to come. Birthdays are no time for Mom to be superwoman—not even when there are 12 four-year-olds in the dining room having a birthday party and your pre-teen announces he has just invited his scout troop over for a snack!

PLAN FOR THE OCCASION

Birthday parties should be fun for parents, too. As one expert party planner stated it, "Plan it small, plan it short, plan it simple—but *plan* it." And plan it as healthy as possible. Don't undo all of your nutritional accomplishments.

Plan Who is Coming

Don't do as I did on Judi's first birthday. Twenty-one one-year-olds were invited (who also brought along their parents) on a cold December afternoon. Be sure to consider your space and how many you can handle easily and comfortably. Keeping the party manageable is essential for a successful celebration.

The birthday boy or girl should not be lost in the crowd. If you feel that you have to include all 24 from the child's class at school in your celebration, why not send a special treat to school for all to share instead of having a party at home?

Send out invitations for a smaller party at home based on a theme for the party and give all the details. Generally invitations to a child's party should be sent out two weeks in advance.

Whatever the style of your party, it should be fun, sincere and relaxed. The secret ingredient to successful entertaining is a warm, friendly hostess who enjoys making everyone feel special. The pleasure of your guests and the joy of being with friends comes before food, decorations and neatness of the house.

Plan the Theme for the Party

Ask your child what kind of party he wants and plan it together around a favorite hobby or sport to carry out the theme. Decide on suitable decorations and favors.

Decorations do not have to be elaborate but will contribute to the festive mood. Tie a bunch of balloons on the mailbox or on the front porch or patio as an obvious sign that this is the place of the celebration. Instead of using place cards at the table, tie a balloon to the back of each guest's chair. Each balloon should carry the name of a guest, written with felt-tip marker.

Favors are as important as the food for young children and these are generally presented as the children leave as a momento of the party.

Plan the Activities

Give the parents a closing time so they will know when to return for their children. Then schedule all the activities so the party will conclude very close to that time.

Plan for one or two games until everyone arrives, or have something special going on such as a clown act or outdoor activities. Small children like to open their gifts as soon as possible and a place should be set up to display the gifts.

Follow the refreshments with a quiet story read aloud which will help children calm down before returning home.

PLAN FOR THE FOOD

For Birthdays

What foods can be served at birthday celebrations that will not cause kids to get overloaded on sugar? For young children the birthday cake is connected to sweetness and love—the highlight of the celebration. But cakes do not have to be loaded with sugar and gooey with thick frosting to be delicious or effective for blowing out the candles.

Commercial cakes are usually loaded with saturated fat, sugar, emulsifiers and stabilizers, unless you are fortunate enough to live near a bakery that bakes with low-fat milk, vegetable oil and reduced sugar. The cakes you make at home can be filled with sweetness and "nutritious love," as Dr. Lendon Smith says.

Best ideas for cakes are:
● Carrot or fresh apple cake with a cream cheese (skim-milk) frosting using pureed fruit.
● Pineapple cake.
● Gingerbread.
● Ice cream cakes. (Made with a healthy ice cream and usually not as sweet as regular cakes.)
● Pumpkin cake.
● Date nut cake.
● Angel food cake (served with assorted fruit toppings, let the kids select their favorite).
● "Mini" cakes such as muffins or cupcakes with unsweetened tinted coconut on top. Place a candle in the center of each muffin.
● Tart shells, meringue cups, or ice cream cones can be filled with custard, lemon or vanilla yogurt and fresh strawberries, peaches or bananas. Top with a

dollop of whipped cream, strawberry, red grapes or slivered almonds.

For Holidays

For celebrations throughout the year try these alternatives:

● *Healthy Heart Buffet.* Let every child bring a favorite fresh fruit from home. Arrange the fruit in bite-size servings so that everyone gets a taste. Serve a cheese or tofu fondue with plenty of bread sticks for dippers. Prepare take home favors of baggies of popcorn or nut mix.

Tofu Cheese Fondue

1 cup tofu, cut up; ½ cup low-fat milk; 1 cup sharp Cheddar cheese, coarsely grated; ½ cup Swiss cheese, coarsely grated; 2 tablespoons Parmesan cheese, grated; ¼ teaspoon dry mustard; apple slices; cubes of whole grain bread.

Place tofu and milk in blender and blend until thick and smooth. Transfer to top of double boiler. Stir in cheeses and mustard. Heat over simmering water until cheeses are melted. Beat smooth with a wire whisk or return to blender. Blend a few seconds until shiny and smooth. Serve warm in a fondue pot with apple slices and bread cubes for dunking.

Keeps a week in the refrigerator. Yields 2 cups.

● *Great Pizza Party.* "We make pizzas," wrote one child about a pizza party. "Mom supplies the dough mix, sauce, cheeses, mushrooms, green peppers, and assorted vegetables. She makes chef hats for everyone to wear and which each takes home. First we mix the dough and knead it—everybody gets a chance—then we put it somewhere warm to rise. Then we cut up the vegetables and grate the cheese. When the dough's ready, we flatten it into little pans—one for each child—and spread the pizza sauce over them. Each child chooses his own toppings. Mom puts all our pizzas in the oven and when they are done, we eat them."

● *An Autumn Party.* Make apple juice or cider popsicles by freezing the juice in paper cups until almost solid. Then insert a popsicle stick and finish freezing.

For taste pleasers serve apple crisp or frozen yogurt banana splits. You supply the frozen yogurt, bananas and toppings and leave the rest up to the kids. Give each child individual cups or bags of one of the following:

Nuts

Wheat or corn kernels

Beef or fruit jerky

Cheese & crackers

Sunflower seeds

Granola

Low sugar cereals in boxes

As favors, give non-edibles such as new pencils, erasers, plastic toys, balloons, shiny new pennies, writing pads, note stationery, sticker seals, plastic watches, etc.

● *A Circus Party.* At each place setting have assorted tiny souffle cups filled with bits of pimiento, olives, raisins, grapes, nuts, cheese, strawberries, red or green peppers and carrot curls (for "hair"). On each plate have the beginning of a bunny salad (or other animal "originals")—a drained pear half (flat side down) on a bed of lettuce. The kids can create their own salads using their favorite ingredients.

Pass a plate of bite-size peanut butter sandwiches to eat with the salad. Have a cupcake for dessert.

Carry out the circus theme with lots of balloons and streamers. Invite the kids to come dressed as clowns, or provide washable makeup and let the kids do their own "clowning."

Sew together bean bags that the kids can toss into different containers. Set up a ring toss. Let kids toss a ball or water balloon into a chalk circle. Set up a treasure hunt to find treats or small toys.

● *A Super Hero Party for the All Stars.* For a cook-out of hamburgers or hot dogs (nitrite-free chicken or turkey) include a vegetable dip for dunking broccoli spears, sweet potato rounds (raw), cauliflowerettes or celery sticks.

Or, if you want to serve the crowd and not work so hard, put out a spread of fun sandwich fillings, baskets of breads, rolls and relishes so everyone can make their own sandwiches. Submarines or hero sandwiches, using a variety of breads, are always favorites. Top a hot chili taco with slivers of red, yellow or green peppers, chilies, asparagus, cucumber slices, or red onion rings. Serve a cold taco filled with unpeeled apple slices, chicken or shrimp salad with tomatoes, orange sections or hard-cooked eggs. Taco sauce is optional.

Meatloaf shaped like a football or basketball makes a score with Superstars. Or try baking individual meat-loaves in muffin tins. Decorate with "faces" or cheese bits put on at the end of baking.

● *A Blue Jean Brunch.* Teens will enjoy this brunch when everyone comes in their favorite jeans.

Menu Ideas

Blue Jean Brunch:

Cold Spicy Chicken
Tuna Cannellini Spread
Marinated Vegetables
Apple Muffins
Fruit Float

South of the Border
   Fiesta

Guacamole Dip with
   Tacos or Corn Chips
Vita Tostada
Fresh Fruit and Yogurt

Vita Tostada

12 thin corn tortillas—bake at 400° for 5 minutes or until crisp
1 pound ground cooked turkey
1 cup tomato sauce
2 tablespoons minced onion
2 teaspoons chili powder
1 teaspoon oregano
¼ teaspoon garlic powder
1 head shredded lettuce
1 cup chopped tomato
1 cup grated sharp Cheddar cheese

Mix the first six ingredients together in a saucepan and simmer for 5 minutes. Divide among the 12 tortillas. Sprinkle the lettuce, tomato and cheese on top of the turkey mixture. Serves 12.

TOTABLE PICNIC FARES

For munching a bunch on picnics, backpacking or in treehouses, pack a totable kid pleaser.

1. Core an apple to within ½ inch of the bottom. Carve out the top to make a little well about 1½ inches across. Fill the cavity with some cottage cheese. Pack a plastic spoon or fork with this salad. (You can scoop out and fill a tomato with cottage cheese, too.)

2. Fill 4-inch pieces of celery stalks, washed and dried, with low fat cream cheese. Sprinkle with paprika—red ants on a log!

3. Fill 4-inch pieces of celery stalks, washed and dried, with plain or crunchy peanut butter, then press in raisins here and there—bugs on a log!

4. Make "mini-kabobs" on wooden picks by alternating cubes of cheese with drained pineapple chunks,

bananas, apples, strawberries or any other fruit. Dates, dried apricots or pitted prunes are also good. Dip fruit slices (avocado, bananas, apples, etc.) in pure lemon juice or orange juice to keep them from turning brown. The fruit keeps for hours.

5. Pack a handful of vegetable snacks as thirst quenchers: carrot curls, celery sticks, radishes and green pepper strips.

6. Take along plastic bags of Nibble Mix, a combination of colorful popcorn, wheat bites, and oat cereal.

Nibble Mix

¼ cup unpopped popcorn
2 cups bite-size shredded wheat
2 cups toasted oat cereal
2 tablespoons oil
¼ cup grated Parmesan cheese
1 tablespoon chili powder or curry powder

Place unpopped popcorn in a heavy skillet or popcorn maker without any oil. Cover skillet with a tight lid and shake pan constantly until all corn is popped. Place popped corn, wheat squares and oat cereal on a baking pan and heat in 300° oven for about 5 minutes. Remove. Drizzle with oil. Combine cheese and chili powder. Sprinkle over corn and stir. Makes about 6 cups.

PLAN FOR THE CLEANUP

Following whatever kind of party you choose to have, ask for volunteers to help with the cleanup chores. Even little kids enjoy putting all the papers and ribbons away.

Whether you serve on paper plates or with ruffles and flourishes, remember that love and good times go together. Your children can lead the way for others to enjoy healthier foods. Help them develop in the way **you** choose.

10
Start Now with Your New Health Goals

Start now—take the first steps toward changing your family's lifestyle to one of better health. Our bodies have been fearfully and wonderfully made by a God who is so caring and precise in the area of His creation that He would not create us without providing a blueprint for us to follow.

Gradually begin where you are and take one step at a time to make improvements. With love and faith, look to Jesus for guidance and knowledge. And remember, with God's help, all things are possible. God weaves the pattern and out of everything some good comes. He has the tools to shape us and make us whole.

Ask God for guidance and direction toward your new goals and way of life. Be ready to respond to the Lord without delay as you pursue these dynamic changes in your own life and those of your family members.

WELLNESS—A WAY OF LIFE

Dedication to your new health goals requires discipline. Each morning, when you start your day with God, write down one goal toward better nutrition that you want to work toward that day. God will provide the strength for you to meet this goal. You may not keep your agreement perfectly every day, but don't let this cause you to take a detour. Just be certain that you start again. Each time you keep an agreement between yourself and God, you become a stronger person.

God's cornerstones for the whole-person approach to wellness include more than just learning how to eat right. Wellness encompasses all of those aspects of one's lifestyle that contribute to physical, mental, emotional and spiritual well-being. Nutrition, exercise, stress management, developing a sense of purpose and a positive self-esteem are all vital elements for optimal health.

Points to Consider

● The nutritional information presented to you in this book will start you on the pathway to better health.

● Exercise for cardio-vascular fitness, strength, endurance and flexibility. Exercise serves as an emotional thermostat by releasing tensions and pulling you out of the slumps. Start slowly and set realistic goals. Stick with your exercise program and build up gradually until it becomes a self-motivating habit. Depress your appetite and control weight through enjoyable means of exercise.

● Managing stress begins with recognizing the fact that a certain degree of stress is normal. It is too much stress or the wrong kind of stress that causes your heart to accelerate, blood pressure to rise, muscles to contract, and the digestive system to close down. Irrational behavior, depression, anxiety, insomnia, headaches, overeating or loss of appetite are also signs of stress. Stressful situations trigger your body's alarm system and cause nutrients to be depleted, nerve energy to be lost, hormonal output to be slowed, and eventually a general state of toxemia exists. Be aware of your body's warning signs.

● A positive self-image stimulates the mind and rejuvenates the body. Attitude alone can work miracles. The Bible tells us *"...be ye transformed by the renewing of your mind..."* (Romans 12:2), and also advises that as a person thinks in his heart, so is he (Proverbs 23:7).

Stress Stoppers

1. Change your perspective. Much psychological distress occurs when your mind irrationally convinces your body that some awful threat is going to befall you. With God's help learn to turn your stressful mountain into a psychological molehill.

Don't demand perfection from everyone. Don't demand approval from everyone. Don't label life's major inconveniences as catastrophes. Don't try everything alone. Don't get angry if others aren't perfect, or do things the way you do.

2. Rest. At home, get sufficient sleep; take naps. At work, take rest and stretch breaks.

3. Get a physical checkup. Make sure your body is ready and capable of providing work. When you've paid for good medical advice, use it.

4. Keep your nutrition sound. Reduce or eliminate nutritionless, simulated, artificial or imitation junk food.

5. Don't overmedicate or overindulge. Drugs, alcohol, tobacco and binge eating only mask symptons. Stress remains and erodes your health. You avoid learning to cope, and are left with the destructive side-effects of substance abuse.

6. Exercise. Enhance your strength and stamina through weight training and aerobic conditioning. The Apostle Paul knew that exercise was important not only for the body but for the spirit. He often used it as an illustration: *"Know ye not that they which run in a race run all, but one receiveth the prize? So run, that ye may obtain... I therefore so run, not as uncertainly... But I keep my body and bring it into subjection..."* (I Corinthians 9:24,26,27).

7. Take control of your time. Make a list of tasks to be done and schedule enough time to do them. Do it now.

8. Pace yourself. Eliminate unnecessary tasks. Some problems are best resolved by neglect.

9. Assert yourself. Don't let your desires, important opinions and reactions go unexpressed. If you want it, ask for it. If you don't like some things, say so. Ask your spouse for affection or your boss for a raise.

10. Take time each day to do relaxation exercises, meditate, listen to music, laugh with a child, pray and study, read the Bible, and turn to God.

WELLNESS—YOUR RESPONSIBILITY

The key ingredient for beginning a new health program for your family is *you*—you must make those decisions that promote wellness. Learning how to eat for health is a responsibility Christians should not take lightly. When God created man, He gave him food and provided him with a home. His third provision was in giving man the power of choice—which we need to put to work in order to receive spiritual and physical blessings. It is my prayer that you will be choosy about the food you put into your body and provide for those you love.

The choice is yours. The care and feeding of healthy kids starts with you.

SOURCES

Eating Well Can Help Your Child Learn Better. This International Reading Association's nutrition brochure is available in quantities of 100 for $4.00, prepaid. Single copies are free by sending a long, self-addressed, stamped envelope to: International Reading Association, P.O. Box 8139, Newark, DE 19711. Topics include: What parents can do to improve the nutrition of children, good nutrition for the brain, energy for learning, suggested reading material, and a nutritional chart of food sources.

Gardens for All. 180 Flynn Avenue, Burlington, VT. 05401. (802) 863-1308. Excellent gardening materials are available from this source.

Guilt-Free Snacking. Yvonne G. Baker. The book may be ordered from your local Christian bookstore or directly from Accent Books, P.O. Box 15337, Denver, CO 80215. 1983.
Guilt-Free Fast Foods. Yvonne G. Baker. Accent Books. 1984.
Guilt-Free Cooking. Yvonne G. Baker. Accent Books. 1985.

Improving Your Child's Behavior Chemistry. Lendon S. Smith, M.D. This book may be ordered from Pocket Books, Simon and Schuster, 1230 Avenue of the Americas, New York, N.Y. 10020. 1977.

Newsletter, School Kit and Video Cassette by Sara Sloan. Order from Sara Sloan, P.O. Box 13824, Atlanta, GA 30324.

Nutritioning Parents Newsletter—Not for everyone, only those who want to feel good. 12 issues for $15.00 in U.S., $18.00 in Canada.

School Kit, containing cassette tapes—30 minutes each.
  (1) Better Food for Better Learning—How to get nutrition served at school.
  (2) Weaning Your Kids from Junk Food—Gradually and with love.
  (3) Booklet—"Turn Can't into Can or How to Get Healthy School Meals."
  (4) Resource Sheet and Articles.

Total kit cost: $14.95

Video Cassette
Nutrition Naturally. Features classroom nutrition projects. Available VHS—¾" or ½" cassette.

Total cassette cost: $59.95

BIBLIOGRAPHY

Adams, Catherine and Richardson, Martha. *Nutritive Value of Foods*. United States Department of Agriculture, Home and Garden Bulletin No. 72, Superintendent of Documents, U.S. Printing Office, Washington, D.C. Revised 1981.

Burkitt, Denis, M.D., FRCS, FRS. *Eat Right to Keep Healthy and Enjoy Life More*. Arco Publishing Co., Inc., New York, N.Y. 1979.

Coffin, Lewis A., M.D. *Children's Nutrition*. Capra Press, Santa Barbara, CA. 1984.

Friday, Sandra K. and Hurwitz, Heidi S. *The Food Sleuth Handbook*. Atheneum, New York, N.Y. 1982.

Myers, John A., M.D. and Schutte, Karl H., Ph.D. *Metabolic Aspects of Health*. Discovery Press, Kenfield, CA. 1979.

National Institutes of Health, Consumer Development Conference Statement, *Health Implications of Obesity*. U.S. Department of Health and Human Services, Public Health Services, Bethesda, MD. 1985.

Smith, Lendon, M.D. *Improving Your Child's Behavior Chemistry*. Pocket Books, New York, N.Y. 1976. *Foods for Healthy Kids*. McGraw-Hill, Inc., New York, N.Y. 1981.

Verny, Thomas, M.D. and Kelly, John. *The Secret Life of the Unborn Child*. Dell Publishing Company, Inc. New York, N.Y. 1981.

Watt, Bernice K. and Merrill, Annabel L. *Handbook of the Nutritional Contents of Food*. United States Department of Agriculture, Dover Publications, Inc., New York, N.Y. 1975.